Writing:
A Comprehensive
Guide to the
Writing Process

Jean L. Pottle

J. WESTON

WALCH
PUBLISHER

Portland, Maine

> *Dedicated to*
> *Dr. Therese Law*
> *Mentor and Friend*
>
> *Who, when asked if she would be*
> *my advisor,*
> *said,*
> *"I'll take you on."*

User's Guide
to
Walch Reproducible Books

As part of our general effort to provide educational materials that are as practical and economical as possible, we have designated this publication a "reproducible book." The designation means that purchase of the book includes purchase of the right to limited reproduction of all pages on which this symbol appears:

Here is the basic Walch policy: We grant to individual purchasers of this book the right to make sufficient copies of reproducible pages for use by all students of a single teacher. This permission is limited to a single teacher, and does not apply to entire schools or school systems, so institutions purchasing the book should pass the permission on to a single teacher. Copying of the book or its parts for resale is prohibited.

Any questions regarding this policy or requests to purchase further reproduction rights should be addressed to:

Permissions Editor
J. Weston Walch, Publisher
321 Valley Street • P.O. Box 658
Portland, Maine 04104-0658

1   2   3   4   5   6   7   8   9   10
ISBN 0-8251-3857-4

Contents

Chapter 4: Writing the Rough Draft 31

Chapter 5: Revising 42

Chapter 6: Proofreading 57

Chapter 7: The Final Draft 65

Part II: Audience and Purpose

Part III: Exploring the Writing World

A Final Word: Evaluating Written Work

How to Use This Book

Someone once said, "She who wants to write must write." Simple, but true. Anyone interested in playing a good game of baseball has to practice. The person who wants to excel at swimming must swim. A great chef begins by learning how to boil water. A great writer begins by putting pen to paper or fingers to keys. Are there ways we, as teachers, can help and encourage our students to become better writers? Absolutely! Every profession has its tools of the trade. This book offers you a toolbox full of ideas to use in your classroom to encourage budding Mark Twains, Stephen Kings, and William Shakespeares.

This book may be used in several ways. You may begin at the beginning and work your way through the entire book, or you may pick and choose explanations and activities that seem most helpful. This book can stand alone as a writing text, or it may be used to supplement other materials. Each topic, covered in one or two reproducibles, is designed to stand alone. This means you can use individual sections for introduction, for reference, or for review. Think of this *Toolbook* as an easily accessible desk reference filled with activities and explanations. A quick trip to the copying machine, helpful pages in hand, launches you on your journey to convince those reluctant writers that they can do it.

This *Toolbook* on the writing process is divided into three parts. Part One delves into the writing process, from brainstorming ideas to publishing a final draft. It covers many of the mechanics of successful writing: developing introductory sentences, organizing paragraphs, and so on.

Part Two focuses on audience and purpose. Students will learn that language and style change as both their readers and their reasons for writing change. What doesn't change, however, are the steps writers complete to produce a sound piece of writing.

Part Three offers explanations and activities to help your students write everything from essays and news reports to advertisements and interviews.

Each chapter begins with Teacher Notes, which gives a brief overview of the material covered in the chapter, as well as suggestions for how to introduce the topic. The reproducible student pages in each chapter offer straightforward explanations of topics from paragraph structure to alliteration. Each student section also includes examples to help students understand what is meant, and exercises to practice what they learn. Suggestions on evaluating written work will be found after this unit. The final section of the book contains an answer key.

With *Writing: A Comprehensive Guide to the Writing Process,* you have the tools your students need to become skilled writers.

Part 1: The Writing Process

I can remember my eighth-grade teacher announcing to the class, "Today you are going to write an essay about your goals for the future." With that, he passed out white lined paper, smiled encouragingly, and sat down. That was it! No discussion. No explanation. Nothing! It didn't occur to him that we needed help. After all, I'm sure he thought, we spoke and wrote English. What more did we need?

We needed a lot more, and fortunately for our students, we now know how to meet some of those needs. Before you ask students to do any writing, tell them about your own struggles as a writer. Do you remember returned papers dripping with red ink? (I always comment in black ink; it doesn't seem quite so hurtful.) Do you remember not being able to write the first word of a paper? Do you remember assignments where your teacher offered no guidelines at all? Make it clear to your students that this is not going to happen to them. You are going to be there to cheer them on. In fact, you are going to give them writing strategies that will help them complete any writing assignment.

We can label those strategies "The Writing Process." The process is made up of six steps. Each of the steps below is fully explained later in this book:

The Writing Process

1. Brainstorming—generating ideas
2. Developing sentences and paragraphs
3. Writing the rough draft—organizing paragraphs
4. Revising—clarifying, rewriting, and polishing the material developed during the rough draft step
5. Proofreading—correcting grammar, spelling, and punctuation
6. Writing the finished piece

Whatever you do, don't begin by assigning an essay. Begin with simple sentences. Then move on to a paragraph assignment, and give your students class time to work on each step of the process. In the first unit of this book, most of the assignments are paragraph assignments. As students develop more confidence in their abilities, you will be able to expand their assignments. By the time you reach Part Three, some writers will think themselves ready to write a novel or movie script. Good luck.

Name _____ Date _____

The Writing Process

Why Write?

Before we look at the first step of the writing process, let's look at the big question: Why write? Believe it or not, there are many reasons. For example,

1. Writing is a fun way to express your ideas for others to read. You are you. No one else can write exactly as you do.

2. Writing is permanent. Our thoughts come and go quickly. When we write something down, it is ours forever.

3. Writing helps us clarify our thoughts.

4. Writing can be edited. You can't change words that have been spoken and heard. What's done is done, no matter what the results. With writing you can rewrite until you get it right!

5. Writing is required for more and more jobs. In fact, many employers ask for a writing sample from prospective employees.

6. Writing is sometimes the only way others know you. If you are communicating via the Internet, your words are you. Think about that.

7. Writing is telling stories. Who knows? You may have a whole new world of stories in your mind that the reading world is waiting for.

8. Writing can be a powerful tool to change minds. Think about historical documents that have altered the way people live. And in the present, writing allows you to express your opinion. A letter to the right person can change your life.

9. Writing closes distances. It gives you a way to communicate with faraway friends.

10. Writing is practical. Learning to write effectively will improve your school performance and your ability to achieve your educational goals.

Chapter 1: Brainstorming

General Introduction

Before students can use the writing process to move from brainstorming to final draft, they must be convinced that they have something worth saying. During the brainstorming step, writers generate as many ideas as possible. These ideas lead first to a general topic and then to a specific writing topic. That is what makes the brainstorming period so vital to the writing process. The ideas listed below will focus your students on the work at hand. Each is simple and fun. You can follow these up with a writing assignment or use them just to calm everyone down before beginning on the day's work.

Brainstorming Strategies

1. Ask students to write a list of words generated by *cereal*. Give them a minute. Ask for volunteers to share lists. After one list has been read, ask if others have similar words on their lists. Usually everyone will mention milk and bowl. As predictable as this is, most students are amazed. Continue by asking for words not mentioned before.

2. Show a photograph. Ask students to generate a word list. Follow the procedure above.

3. Write a famous person's name on your overhead. Ask for words to describe this person. Ask students to share lists.

Although writing is a serious business, it is important that students enjoy the brainstorming session of their writing assignments. If they do, they will enter the rough draft stage with a good deal of confidence.

Early in the school year, you will probably want the entire class to work on the same brainstorming techniques. As time goes by, students should be able to use whatever techniques work for them. For some, it will be a word association strategy, as mentioned above. For others, it may be working with the alphabet, as outlined on page 6. For others, a class discussion of the assigned topic is all that is needed. Encourage students to notice what works for them.

Meeting Special Needs

The brainstorming activities suggested in the following pages can be easily adapted for a variety of teaching situations. If you are working with ESL students, they can complete these brainstorming activities in their own languages, share them with other students or the whole class, and then proceed, with help from their peers, to translate their work into English. This enables everyone to benefit from the language diversity of the classroom.

Students who have very limited abilities can be given words to work with. Generate a list of related words. Write one word per index card. Ask students to organize these words into sentences. These sentences can later be rearranged into paragraphs. You might want to ask some students who enjoy doing word associations to prepare these cards for you.

(continued)

Chapter 1:
Brainstorming *(continued)*

Extension Activity

Constructing a web is another activity students enjoy that helps them to generate ideas. Demonstrating web construction on the board before asking students to do it on their own helps them to visualize how to use this method. To start, draw a large circle on the board. In that circle write a thought-provoking word. Words that usually work are *vacation, homework, report cards, brother/ sister.* Draw a series of lines from your center circle. Ask students to supply descriptive phrases to write on the lines projecting from your circle. Here is an example:

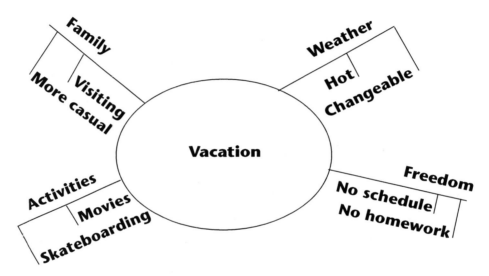

Follow this activity up by asking students to write a descriptive paragraph about the topic. They can use the phrases on the board or write their own.

A Final Word

Whenever you introduce a new brainstorming technique, work through some part of the assignment with the entire class. Be sure to write responses on the board or on an overhead. Writers need words and ideas, and those are what these activities should supply.

As students develop approaches to this stage of the writing process, allow class time for individuals to explain what works for them. You might also want to share what works for you. If possible, students should see you struggling with your own writing, whether it is a memo for the faculty, a report for the school board, or a plan for the class. Too often, students see teachers as experts who never struggle to complete work. A reality check is good for everyone.

Chapter 1: Brainstorming

Spontaneous Generation

 Brainstorming is allowing the free flow of words and/or ideas to generate anything, from the seeds of entirely new creations to the solution to a specific problem. What's acceptable? Any words, any ideas—wacky, weird, or wonderful!

Brainstorming is a great way to start the writing process. The word *process* says it all; a process lists the necessary steps to reach a goal. In this case, your goal is to write. Here are the steps you can take to reach that goal:

Step 1   Brainstorming—generating ideas

Step 2   Developing sentences based on those ideas

Step 3   Writing the rough draft—organizing ideas into paragraphs

Step 4   Revising—clarifying, rewriting, and polishing the material

Step 5   Proofreading—correcting grammar, spelling, and punctuation

Step 6   Writing the finished piece

That's it. A straightforward process. You can do it.

Getting started is hard for all writers. Even the most experienced writer can be terrified of a blank piece of paper. Because brainstorming generates words and ideas to put on that blank sheet, it is the first step in the writing process.

The word *brainstorming* suggests that a storm—wind, rain, snow, sleet—is raging in your brain. There should be a storm, all right: a storm of words. If you just let your brain take over, it can supply you with all kinds of words.

On the surface, this appears to be a fairly easy task. The problem is that most of us get caught up in emotion when we even think about a writing assignment. That emotion is usually **fear**, which keeps us from making any kind of progress. Relaxing and completing some straightforward brainstorming gets us warmed up for writing. Athletes flex their muscles. Writers flex their brains. Remember, the purpose here is playing with words and ideas to help you get started writing.

No matter what you want to write—from a letter to friends to a report—all writing assignments ask for two things: words and ideas. After a little brain flexing, you will be able to come up with both. The rules of the brainstorming game are simple—relax and go with the flow.

Name _____ Date _____

 Exercise 1.1

Here is a "go-with-the-flow" strategy for generating words and ideas. All you have to do is write a word that begins with each of the letters below. Your goal is to get that brain percolating. Once you have words, you are on the way to developing ideas. *A* and *B* are done for you. Remember, there are no wrong answers. What a deal!

(a) answers

(b) bags

(c) _____

(d) _____

(e) _____

(f) _____

(g) _____

(h) _____

(i) _____

(j) _____

(k) _____

(l) _____

(m) _____

(n) _____

(o) _____

(p) _____

(q) _____

(r) _____

(s) _____

(t) _____

(u) _____

(v) _____

(w) _____

(x) _____

(y) _____

(z) _____

Name _____ Date _____

Exercise 1.2

On the list you created for Exercise 1.1, circle two words you use often. Write those words on the following lines. Below each one, list all the words that come to mind when you let your thoughts wander about each word.

Here is an example of what to do using the *A* word.

	Word 1 <u>Answers</u>	
Example	Hard to remember	Too short
	Need to learn	Too long
	Wrong	Written
	Right	Questions

Word 1	**Word 2**
_____	_____
_____	_____
_____	_____
_____	_____
_____	_____

Sometimes it's fun to include opposites on your list—in the case of *answers*, the opposite would be *questions*.

Review

Review your list. Because you began with something familiar, you probably had ideas. You took the first step in finding a subject to write about.

Now that you have warmed up, couldn't you write a paragraph about either one of those words? True, your paragraph might not be ready for publication; but you *could* write it! That is always the first step of the writing process: getting some words—any words—down on paper. Remember this the next time you are writing a letter, taking an exam, or doing any kind of writing. Relax and list. With this list of words, you are ready to think about using these words in sentences. In the second stage of the writing process, you will have a chance to do just that.

Writing: A Comprehensive Guide to the Writing Process

Chapter 2: Sentences and Paragraphs

General Introduction

Once students have proven to themselves that brainstorming helps them come up with words, they are ready to progress to the second step of the writing process: developing sentences and paragraphs. The goal of this step is for students to develop sentences using the word lists generated in Step 1. Once sentences are written, students will be able to see that what began as a random list of words has led to a group of sentences that support a common idea.

Strategies for Developing Sentences and Paragraphs

To demonstrate this to your students, write the following list on your board or overhead.

apples	pears	peaches
trees	pies	picking

This random list was generated from the word *apples*. Ask your students what connections they can find among the words. Mention that not everyone will make the same connections, which is what makes writing and writers unique. Someone may suggest that three types of fruit are men–tioned. Another may volunteer that each of these fruits can be baked in pies. A third may notice that all these fruits must be picked from trees.

Ask your students to write a sentence for each word. They may use more than one of the words in a sentence. The purpose is to get sentences down on paper, with the ulti-

mate goal of developing a paragraph with these sentences. When the students are finished, write the following sentences on your overhead:

- Fresh fruit makes the best pies.
- My favorite fruits grow on trees.
- Picking fruit is the first step to a great pie.

Ask which of these sentences could introduce and connect their sentences. Ask for examples. Have students select one of the sentences and develop a paragraph based on it and using their own sentences.

Meeting Special Needs

Another way to approach sentence writing is to write the words on the board or overhead, divide students into groups of three or four, and ask each group to work on generating sentences. Teaming ESL students with English-speaking students gives the former a safe way to explore language. The more language they see and hear, the better. Students whose language difficulty leaves them silent in full-class discussions will frequently speak up in a small group.

A Final Word

Work on this step of the writing process until you feel students are ready to begin writing rough drafts. Mention to your students that as they practice brainstorming and developing sentences and paragraphs, they are refining strategies applicable to any writing situation.

Chapter 2: Sentences and Paragraphs

From Words to Sentences

 A sentence is a word or group of words expressing a complete thought. It can be a statement.

| **Example** | The cat chased the dog. |

It can be a question.

| **Example** | Are you sure? |

It can even be a one-word command.

| **Example** | Stop! |

It can be a short exclamation.

| **Example** | No way! |

All sentences have a subject—whatever it is that is acting or existing in a certain way—and a verb—the word that expresses the action or state of being of the subject. Even the one-word command above, "Stop!" (verb), has an understood subject—"you." The exclamation "No way!" implies the rest of the sentence: "No way [did the cat chase the dog]!"

 Exercise 2.1

This exercise is an opportunity to play with words. The first column on the next page gives a list of nouns—naming words. The second column is a list of verbs—action words, or words that link subjects to words in the predicate. The third column lists two types of descriptive words, adjectives and adverbs. You can use adjectives to describe nouns. You can use adverbs to describe verbs, adjectives, and other adverbs. For this activity, you can also use the definite and indefinite articles *the, an,* and *a.* Mix and match words from all three lists. How many sentences can you make with these words? List your sentences on the back of this sheet.

| **Example** | The camera has been lost. |

Name _____   Date _____

Nouns	Verbs	Adjectives and Adverbs
camera	fell	slightly
lobster	lost	slowly
musicians	balanced	already
pizza	swim	green
sandwiches	sat	chilled
plate	cried	red
player	was	glorious
computer	played	completely
disks	is	crisp
calendar	has been	sadly
clock	crashed	quickly
watch	watched	cool
graduation	were	awesome
fans	moved	enthusiastic
fashion	seen	fantastic
eyes	walked	good
people	clipped	dreadful

Expanding Sentences with Prepositional Phrases

When you limit the words in your sentences to nouns, verbs, adjectives, adverbs, and articles, you limit the possibility of writing interesting sentences. What makes an interesting sentence? Detail! Not just any old detail, but detail that helps your reader understand what you are trying to say. Read the two sentences that follow. Which do you think is more interesting to read?

Example	The inn was small. "The Jolly Sandboys was a small roadside inn of pretty ancient date." (Charles Dickens, *The Old Curiosity Shop*)

In the first example, all we know is that the inn was small. How small? We don't know. Where is it located? We don't know that, either. In the second example, the author has named the inn and has given us some idea of where it is located and how old it is. Which sentence is more interesting?

Most readers would find the second sentence more interesting than the first. The author added adjectives, as in **small, roadside**, and **ancient**. He also added a prepositional phrase, **of pretty ancient date**. A prepositional phrase is a phrase that starts with a preposition and ends with a

Writing: A Comprehensive Guide to the Writing Process

Name _____ Date _____

noun. Other words, like adjectives and adverbs, can be included between the preposition and the noun. Adding prepositional phrases is a good way to offer additional information, thus making your writing more interesting.

Here is a short list of prepositions that you can use to make prepositional phrases. There are many more, but this list will get you started.

after	by	from	to
at	down	in	through
before	during	of	under
between	for	over	up

Exercise 2.2

Use this list of prepositions to form at least three prepositional phrases.

Example	between midnight and dawn

_____

_____

_____

_____

Exercise 2.3

These simple sentences don't give the reader much information. Use prepositional phrases to tell the reader something more about the subject of each sentence. (The subject of each sentence is in **bold type**.) Use the list of prepositions above, and any others you can think of.

Example	The **boy** ran.
	The **boy** ran down the maze of narrow streets that led through the town.

1. The **ship** sank.

_____

2. **Traffic** was heavy.

_____

3. **We** ate dinner.

_____

4. **Trees** fell.

_____

Writing: A Comprehensive Guide to the Writing Process

Name _____   Date _____

5. The **computer** crashed.

   _____

6. **He** removed the disk.

   _____

7. The **river** flooded.

   _____

8. The **audience** cheered.

   _____

9. The **fire** burned.

   _____

10. **Musicians** played.

   _____

Combining Sentences and Clauses

You can make sentences more interesting by adding adjectives, adverbs, or prepositional phrases. You can also develop your sentences by adding **clauses**. The biggest difference between prepositional phrases and clauses is that prepositional phrases never have both subjects and verbs, while clauses always have both.

Example	**Prepositional phrase:** After the rain **Clause:** Rain fell

You may think that the definition of a clause is very similar to the definition of a sentence—and you'd be right. Some clauses can be sentences. But a sentence always makes sense without any help, and some clauses don't. A clause that makes sense by itself is called an **independent clause.**

Example	Rain fell

A clause that needs something else to make it work as a sentence is called a **dependent clause.**

Example	While the rain fell

Dependent clauses often start with words like these:

after	since	where
although	that	which
because	unless	while
if	when	who

Writing: A Comprehensive Guide to the Writing Process

Name _____   Date _____

 Exercise 2.4

Practice adding clauses to simple sentences. Combine the simple sentences on the left with the clauses on the right to form new sentences. Write your new sentences on the back of this sheet, or on another piece of paper.

Example	After she floated down the river, she ate an entire pizza.

Simple sentences	**Clauses**
The students walked.	After we met
Fifteen fish were caught.	Unless I am wrong
I finished my assignment.	While they were sleeping
The lecture lasted an hour.	Although it is raining
My alarm clock works.	While he ate pie
The building collapsed.	Who should have known better
The mail carrier delivered letters.	After mowing the lawn
They started without me.	Which is a waste of time
She ate an entire pizza.	Who wore a hat and wig
I will attend the meeting.	Because it was tired
Families can be helpful.	When they try
Charles Dickens wrote *Great Expectations*.	After she floated down the river
I could have danced all night.	Since it was made of green cheese
California is called The Sunshine State.	While I played the guitar
Traveling to another country could be interesting.	If you know what I mean
Friends can be a pain.	Although I had no bait

Name _____ Date _____

Creating Sentence Variety

Descriptive words, prepositional phrases, and clauses are three ways to make your sentences interesting. But if you always use the same approach in your sentences, readers will lose interest. You don't always need to put adjectives and adverbs in front of the words they describe. The same is true of phrases and clauses. Varying the structure of your sentences makes your writing more interesting to read.

Example	He saw a fire through the window. It was glowing.
	He saw a fire, which was glowing, through the window.
	He saw a glowing fire through a window.
	Through a window he saw a glowing fire.
	He saw, through a window, a glowing fire.
	As he looked through a window, he saw a glowing fire.
	The fire, which he saw through a window, was glowing.

If you connect two complete thoughts with the conjunctions "and" or "but," you must place a comma before the conjunction. This sentence is made up of two complete thoughts, so it needs a comma before "and:"

| **Example** | Two students met at the park, and they shared their lunches. |

This sentence is a simple sentence, so it needs no comma:

| **Example** | Two students met at the park and shared their lunches. |

 Exercise 2.5

Rewrite these sentences by moving phrases and clauses. Combine ideas by using phrases and clauses. Remember to use commas if you use "and" or "but" to connect two complete thoughts. Write each sentence in as many different ways as you can.

1. Juan held a black book in his hands. He talked with a friend._____

    _____

    _____

    _____

2. Erin was pleased. The concert was not canceled. _____

    _____

    _____

    _____

Writing: A Comprehensive Guide to the Writing Process

Name _____   Date _____

3. Karl walked by the door. The door was open. A man watched him. _____

_____

_____

_____

4. Lyle is alone. The house is deserted. The wind is howling. _____

_____

_____

_____

5. I walked around the lake. I saw a large bird. It sat on a rock. _____

_____

_____

_____

From Sentences to Paragraphs

 A paragraph is a group of sentences linked together by a common idea. An introductory or topic sentence tells your reader what you plan to write about in the paragraph, and the other sentences provide material supporting the idea introduced.

Read the following paragraph from a speech, "New England Weather," given by Mark Twain in 1876. Notice his introductory sentence. Then see how he supports the idea of changeable New England weather.

There is a sumptuous variety about the New England weather that compels the stranger's admiration—and regret. The weather is always doing something there; always attending strictly to business; always getting up new designs and trying them on people to see how they will go. But it gets through more business in Spring than in any other season. In the Spring I have counted one hundred and thirty-six different kinds of weather inside of twenty-four hours.

Does Mark Twain support the idea that New England weather is varied? He certainly does! You can use the same approach to develop your own paragraphs.

Let's say your teacher has asked you to write a paragraph about a familiar object. First you brainstorm a list of words. These may be naming words, action words, descriptive words, or a combination of word types. You decide to work with the letter *b* to see where that takes you. One possible list includes:

bags	briefcases
backpacks	bologna
books	baggage

      Writing: A Comprehensive Guide to the Writing Process

Name _____   Date _____

Okay. What now? Can you find any connections linking these words to a common idea? Try putting them in sentences:

- Bags are for carrying things, like bologna sandwiches.

- Briefcases hold papers.

- Baggage brings my stuff with me when I travel.

- Backpacks carry books or camping gear.

Does a connection link these words? You bet. Every word on your list is either a container of some sort or something to be carried in those containers.

What now? The next step is to write a sentence stating the connection you have found.

Examples	It is almost impossible to carry the supplies you need for one day without some type of bag. Or: Bags come in a variety of sizes, shapes, and colors. Or: Although we take bags for granted, where would we be without them?

There are lots of other possibilities. Notice that each of these introductory sentences routes your writing in quite a different way.

- Sentence 1 will lead to a paragraph about the ways in which bags are used.

- Sentence 2 will lead to a paragraph about different types of bags.

- Sentence 3 will lead to a paragraph about why people need bags.

It's up to you to choose whichever will work best for you.

Once you have picked an introductory sentence, you must decide which of your original sentences will continue the idea stated in your introductory sentence. You may find that you need completely new sentences. That's fine. The old ones have done their job: They have led you to a subject for your paragraph on a familiar object.

Here's a quick review of the second step of the writing process.

1. Brainstorm a list of words.

2. Use them in sentences.

3. Look for a link.

4. If there is no obvious link, add words to your list until you can make some connections.

5. Write an introductory sentence.

Name _____ Date _____

Exercise 2.6

Write a paragraph based on the example discussed on pages 15–16.

_____

_____

_____

_____

_____

_____

_____

_____

Exercise 2.7

This activity will give you further practice writing sentences that support a common, or main, idea. As you move through the steps of the writing process, developing related sentences and linking them to a common idea will become easier.

1. Write the names of four of your favorite television shows on the four main lines on the left.

2. Next to each title, on the lines to the right, write two reasons you like the show. Think about such things as believable characters, lots of action, good music, mystery, humor, educational content, interesting people. When you have finished, check to see if there

  Writing: A Comprehensive Guide to the Writing Process

Name _____ Date _____

are any similarities among your reasons. If so, you have found a link. You have a way of explaining why you like specific programs. You can now write sentences about the shows explaining why you like them.

Examples	Two of my favorite shows are "Today" and "Oprah."
	The hosts of these two shows always have up-to-date information on everything from fashion to movie stars.
	Katie and Oprah interview all kinds of interesting people.
	I hear neat music on both shows.

Now it's your turn. Write four sentences about your favorite TV shows on the lines below.

_____

_____

_____

_____

The first sentence in the example introduces an idea that the other sentences support. Write such a sentence to introduce your sentences. Now, review your sentences. Decide which should come first, second, third, and last. It is up to you to decide what is the most logical arrangement.

Believe it or not, you are now ready to write the rough draft of a paragraph. A rough draft is your first attempt at putting a group of sentences together into a paragraph. On a separate sheet of paper, write a paragraph about your favorite television programs.

Review

Let's review the steps you followed in the preceding exercise so you can apply them to other writing situations.

1. List related subjects.

2. List reasons for your interest in these subjects.

3. Write your reasons in sentences.

4. Decide what links your ideas. Write a sentence expressing this link.

5. Determine the sequence for your sentences.

6. Rewrite your sentences as a paragraph.

Name _____ Date _____

Exercise 2.8

Follow the steps you reviewed above using one of these topics:

1. Famous people
2. Professional sports teams
3. Songs or movies
4. Cars

_____

_____

_____

_____

_____

_____

_____

_____

_____

Chapter 3: Literary Devices

General Introduction

Authors use figurative language for a variety of reasons: to help the reader "see" what the writing is showing, to increase the impact of what the writer is saying, to express something in a fresh new way. In this section, students will become aware of the important literary devices of alliteration, sensory language, irony, simile, metaphor, onomatopoeia, and personification. They will learn to identify these devices, and to use them in their own writing.

Strategies for Using Figurative Language

To show students the richness figurative language can add, write this sentence on the board or overhead:

He had a big nose.

Ask students how clear a picture they have of this person and his nose. Point out that you could change the adjective modifying the noun—enormous, gigantic—but the reader still wouldn't know that much more about the person's nose. You can use devices like metaphor, simile,and personification to make the image much stronger. Write the following sentences on the board or over- head:

The mountain crest of his nose split his face into two continents.

His nose seemed to travel before him, like a scout before an exploring party.

His nose lived in one zip code, while he lived in another one.

Ask students what picture these sentences give of the person's face. Explain that the first sentence uses metaphor, the second uses simile, and the third uses personification.

Encourage students to start a collection of literary devices they see in books they read, in advertising, and in other written sources.

Meeting Special Needs

Students with special needs should be asked to concentrate on one literary device at a time. Have them practice creating allit- eration with the help of a word list or dictio- nary. ESL students can share—in both the original language and English—examples of these devices in their first language.

A Final Word

The literary devices covered in this section will help students bring their writing to life. But remember, they must be used sparingly. If every sentence in a piece of writing uses a simile or metaphor, readers can be left wondering just what the subject of the piece is.

Chapter 3: Literary Devices

Language—Figurative and Literal

Have you ever said "get lost" to someone? Did you really mean that you wanted the person to lose her way? Of course not. You just wanted her to go away from you. "Get lost" is an example of **figurative language**. When our words mean exactly what they say, as in "Pass the salt, please," we are using **literal language**. Figurative language is language that calls on the writer and the reader to think more creatively, to use their imaginations.

Examples	The exam was a piece of cake. She is as slow as cold molasses. My brother eats like a horse. Mimi is as skinny as a scarecrow. She eats like a bird. This will take forever.

Here are the literal meanings of the figurative sentences above.

The exam was easy.

She is very slow.

My brother eats a lot.

Mimi is very thin.

She eats very little.

This will take a great deal of time.

Writers use figurative writing to jazz up their words and to encourage readers to use their imaginations. There are many types of figurative language. In this section, we will look at a few of the most useful ones:

alliteration	metaphor	simile
imagery	onomatopoeia	
irony	personification	

Name _____ Date _____

Alliteration

 Alliteration is the use of the same letter or the same sound at the beginning of two or more words that are near each other.

Alliteration can emphasize the sound being repeated. It can also give words a strong rhythm. For example, in Alfred Tennyson's poem "The Eagle," the poet uses alliteration to describe an eagle on a rocky outcropping:

He **clasps** the **crag** with **crooked** hands.

Notice how the repeated "c" sounds affect the line. The meaning is the same as "He holds the cliff with his talons," but the effect is much more striking.

 Exercise 3.1

Each of the following sentences includes alliteration. Underline the alliterative words.

1. He moved swiftly and silently through the night.
2. As the day dawned, I thought with dread of the morning's exam.
3. We tramped through fens, past farmland, toward the distant hills.
4. Flavia was delayed, but not deterred.
5. The rioters ripped through the city center.

Writing: A Comprehensive Guide to the Writing Process

Name _____ Date _____

Exercise 3.2

Now create some alliteration yourself. Add an alliterative word at some point in each of the following sentences.

Example	The sign moved in the wind.
	The sign swung in the wild wind.

1. The forest trees quietly swayed back and forth.

   _____

   _____

2. There were twelve different kinds of ice cream listed.

   _____

   _____

3. Mr. Lu rushed home through the heavy traffic.

   _____

   _____

4. The frightened bank clerk dropped to his knees as the alarm sounded.

   _____

   _____

While alliteration can be fun, it's important not to overuse it. Many tongue-twisters could be described as extreme alliteration.

Example	Peter Piper picked a peck of pickled peppers.

To keep your writing from sounding like a tongue-twister, use alliteration sparingly.

Name _____   Date _____

Imagery

 Imagery is figurative language that appeals to the senses of the reader: taste, touch, sight, smell, and hearing. Carefully chosen words can help your readers "see" or "hear" what you are describing.

Examples	**Sight:** The square of sky I saw through my window changed from the night's flat velvet black to the shot-silk grey of early dawn, that lustrous grey that suggests the sunrise soon to come.
	Smell: The air was rich with the sweet, yeasty essence of new bread, tickling the nostrils, making the mouth water.
	Sound: As the truck lumbered over the bridge, the old boards creaked and groaned under its weight.

 Exercise 3.3

Practice using imagery by adding "sensory" words to the following sentences.

Example	We heard the bells.
	The jangling bells chimed the hour.

1. The rusty gate was noisy.

   _____

2. The pizza was hot.

   _____

3. They jumped into the river.

   _____

4. The machinery was noisy.

   _____

5. We heard the sound of traffic.

   _____

6. Cobwebs covered the entrance to the cave.

   _____

7. Ricardo walked toward the house.

   _____

Name _____ Date _____

Irony

 Irony is a figure of speech in which the literal meaning (the word-for-word meaning) is the opposite of the author's intended meaning.

At first glance, this may seem to make little sense. Still, we use and hear irony every day. Have you ever lost something you needed and said, "Well, this is great, isn't it"? Did you really mean that what happened was good? Of course you didn't. You meant just the opposite. You were using irony.

Read the paragraph below. Underline the words that are meant to be ironic.

Marie learned the hard way that not all friends can be trusted. She had not meant to tell her secret to anyone. In a moment of weakness and hoping for understanding, she told Angelica. Later she learned that Angelica had repeated it. Now, after two days, everyone in school knew. "What a great friend Angelica is," she thought.

If you underlined the last sentence, you are absolutely right. Angelica was not a great friend. The writer meant just the opposite of what she wrote.

 Exercise 3.4

Underline the examples of irony in the following sentences and explain why each is ironic.

1. As Monica finished the huge stack of work she said, "That was a good time!"
   Ironic because: _____

2. "Oh, wonderful," Lloyd said, as the lightning and thunder moved closer.
   Ironic because: _____

3. The lionhearted hunter was frightened by the mouse that darted between his feet.
   Ironic because: _____

4. The runner arrived at home plate to learn that he had never touched first base. His homerun was a "no run."
   Ironic because: _____

5. "It's nothing," Max announced as he turned in his 56-page report.
   Ironic because: _____

    Writing: A Comprehensive Guide to the Writing Process

Name _____ Date _____

Simile

 Similes compare two unlike things, using the form "like a" or "as . . . as."

Example	Kimi's face was as white as a camellia blossom.

Similes work by giving one of the things being compared the characteristics of the other thing. In the example above, we don't know what Kimi's essential characteristics are. But one of the characteristics of a camellia flower is whiteness. By comparing Kimi's face and a camellia flower, this simile is saying, "Kimi's face was absolutely white." In fact, a girl's face would never really be as white as a flower, but the simile helps us visualize her face as unusually white, whiter than a face should be. The same is true in similes like "biceps like a rock," or "hands soft as thistledown." The comparison lends one thing the essential characteristics of another thing.

Read this excerpt from Charles Dickens's *A Christmas Carol*. Notice Dickens's use of similes in his description of Scrooge. Underline each simile.

Oh! But he was a tight-fisted hand at the grindstone was Scrooge! A squeezing, wrenching, grasping, scraping, clutching, covetous old sinner! Hard and as sharp as flint, from which no steel had ever struck out generous fire; secret and self-contained, and solitary as an oyster. . . .

Do you see how Dickens used words with distinct characteristics in his comparisons?

 Exercise 3.5

Practice identifying the essential characteristics of things. List as many characteristics as you can for each word below.

Example	concrete—hard, grey, waterproof, man-made, moldable, durable

1. spring water _____

2. snow _____

3. knife _____

4. asphalt _____

5. granite _____

Writing: A Comprehensive Guide to the Writing Process

Name _____ Date _____

 Exercise 3.6

Now try to think of things that have the essential characteristics of these adjectives.

Example	dry—dust, sand, desert, wind

1. wet _____
2. cold_____
3. hard _____
4. thick _____
5. gentle _____

 Exercise 3.7

Now choose words to complete the similes below. Find nouns with the characteristics you want to suggest in your comparison.

Example	Grass is like a **blanket covering the earth**.

1. The child was as thoughtful as_____ .
2. Summer is like_____ .
3. The moon is like _____ .
4. The weather is as changeable as _____ .
5. Friendship is like _____ .
6. Good friends are like _____ .
7. Her remarks are as sharp as _____ .
8. He ran as fast as _____ .
9. The book is as dull as _____ .

Overused Similes

Like other figures of speech, similes can be overused. Some similes have been used so often that they have lost their freshness. Similes like the ones listed here are so overused that they won't add anything to your writing. Avoid them, and look for fresh comparisons of your own.

Overused Similes	
as strong as an ox	as slow as molasses
as wise as an owl	as pretty as a picture
as pale as a ghost	as quiet as a mouse

Writing: A Comprehensive Guide to the Writing Process

Name _____   Date _____

Metaphor

 A metaphor is a figure of speech in which the writer implies a comparison between two quite different things.

Metaphors and similes are very similar. They both compare two unlike things. To keep them separate, remember that similes always include the word "like" or "as."

| **Example** | **Simile:** The darkness enfolded the village **like** a blanket. |
| | **Metaphor:** The village was blanketed in darkness. |

A well-known line from Shakespeare's play *As You Like It* is a good example of metaphor. In this quotation, Shakespeare compares the world to a play in which people play their parts.

> All the world's a stage,
> And all the men and women merely
>   players.
> They have their exits and their
>   entrances. . . .

Read the paragraph below and underline the metaphor. Here Washington Irving is describing Rip van Winkle's very difficult wife.

A tart tongue never mellows with age, and a sharp tongue is the only edged tool that grows keener with constant use.

(Washington Irving, *Rip van Winkle*)

Did you underline the entire passage? If not, look back at the quotation and ask yourself why Irving uses the adjective "tart." He was comparing the tongue first to a piece of fruit, which can be either sweet or tart. Later he compares Mrs. van Winkle's tongue to a sharpened tool. Obviously, Rip's wife is often angry.

 Exercise 3.8

Write an explanation of each metaphor below by first identifying the objects being compared. Next, explain what each metaphor means.

1. He is a tower of strength.

Compares _____ and _____

Meaning: _____

2. The curtain of night fell over the scene.

Compares _____ and _____

Meaning: _____

3. Don't rock the boat.

Compares _____ and _____

Meaning: _____

4. He lives on easy street.

Compares _____ and _____

Meaning: _____

5. They had a whirlwind romance.

Compares _____ and _____

Meaning: _____

Writing: A Comprehensive Guide to the Writing Process

Name _____ Date _____

Onomatopoeia

 Onomatopoeia is the use of words that sound like or suggest the objects or actions being named.

Although the word "onomatopoeia" (pronounced **on**-uh-**mat**-uh-**pea**-yuh) sounds very complex, many of the words that it includes are very simple. Our words for the sounds animals make are often onomatopoeia: moo, neigh, bark.

In his poem "The Bells," Edgar Allan Poe uses onomatopoeia. Underline the words in this excerpt that remind you of the sound of bells.

Hear the sledges with the bells—
　Silver bells!
What a world of merriment their melody foretells!
　How they tinkle, tinkle, tinkle.
　In the icy air of night!
While the stars that oversprinkle
All the Heavens, seem to twinkle
　With a crystalline delight.

If you underlined words like tinkle, oversprinkle, crystalline, you are on the right track.

 Exercise 3.9

Here is a list of nouns and a list of "sound" words. Match the sound word with the appropriate noun.

Example	The fire crackled.

Nouns	Sound Words
a turkey	hissed
water	sizzled
a snake	buzzed
leaves	gurgled
garbage cans	popped
a bee	cawed
a steak	clanged
a balloon	gobbled
a crow	rustled

Writing: A Comprehensive Guide to the Writing Process

Name _____   Date _____

Personification

 Personification is a figure of speech in which the writer gives human qualities to an animal or inanimate object.

You have probably used personification without even knowing it.

Example	This door won't budge.
	I put my book right there; it must have walked away.
	My car refuses to start.

Obviously, no door decides to be stubborn, no book walks away, and cars can't refuse anything. In each case, we have given these objects the ability to think and act. Notice that the first six letters of **personification** spell the word **person**. When you use personification, you are giving the characteristics of a person to an animal or object.

Read the following excerpt from James Stephens' poem "Check." Underline the examples of personification.

> The night was creeping on the ground;
> She crept and did not make a sound
> Until she reached the tree, and then
> She covered it, and stole again
> Along the grass beside the wall.

Throughout this stanza Stephens uses personification to describe night. Notice that the night creeps quietly until "she" reaches a tree that "she" covers. The use of personification creates a picture for the reader. It is language that makes the poem vivid.

 Exercise 3.10

Next to each sentence below, write the noun that has been personified, and the word that describes the noun.

Example	The moon hid her face behind a cloud.
	Answer: moon, hid

1. The moaning trees outside my window kept me awake. _____
   _____

2. Rain slapped against my face. _____

3. My dog Misery asked to go outside. _____

4. Doug's little car waited for him at the door of the gym. _____
   _____

5. Lyle's boat seemed to have a mind of its own as it refused to start. _____
   _____

Writing: A Comprehensive Guide to the Writing Process

Chapter 4:
Writing the Rough Draft

General Introduction

A rough draft is a writer's first attempt to assemble ideas in some logical way. After completing the first two steps of the writing process—brainstorming and developing sentences—students are ready to expand their ideas beyond simple paragraphs. When students write rough drafts, they need not concern themselves with spelling, grammar, or well-written sentences (they will be thrilled to hear this): Their goal is to expand on ideas, to explore a subject thoroughly.

Strategies for Writing Rough Drafts

To help students make the leap from paragraphs to longer pieces, make copies of a well-written editorial from your local newspaper. Find one that investigates a topic familiar to your students—curfews, teenage violence, speed limits, education. Ask your students to read through the editorial, underlining the sentences they feel are most important. Discuss those sentences. Emphasize that a well-written piece enables the reader to see how sentence ideas are linked. Encourage students to suggest other ways in which the editorial might have been written. Tell them that by reading what others write, they become involved in ideas—what writing is all about!

To get them started on writing a rough draft, distribute copies of the guidelines on page 32. Discuss these guidelines, and explain their first assignment. They are to write a two-paragraph response to the edito-

rial they just finished reading. Since discussion is a form of brainstorming, they should be ready to start. To speed students on their way, suggest that the first paragraph explain what the editorial is about. In the second paragraph, students should discuss why they agree or disagree with the article.

Although there is no reason to collect every rough draft your students write, collect this one. By doing so, you are saying, "Rough drafts are important." Read the rough drafts, and make at least one positive comment. Don't correct these drafts. Returned drafts should be kept in individual folders. Students can revisit these drafts at a later time.

Meeting Special Needs

To be sure that all students can read the editorial mentioned above, re-copy it enlarged and double-spaced. Point out to all your students that doing this makes it easier not only to read but to comment on.

Another way of doing this assignment is to project the article on an overhead. That way, you can write in comments. Students who have trouble processing information need to both see and hear.

A Final Word

Ask students to bring in writing they have enjoyed. Discuss the writing with the class.

Name _____ Date _____

Chapter 4: Writing the Rough Draft

Guidelines

 A rough draft is the writer's first, unpolished attempt to arrange sentences into paragraphs organized around a main idea.

1. Double-space your rough draft.

2. If you are using a word processor, be sure you have a disk on which to save your work.

3. Write on only one side of the paper.

4. Number each page of your rough draft in the upper right-hand corner.

5. Do not erase anything from a handwritten rough draft. Merely cross out the words you don't want. If you are using a word processor, you may either erase the words or leave them to be crossed out later. One reason for saving what you have written is that you frequently find that you had it right the first time.

6. Always leave wide margins to allow space for additional information.

7. Do not worry about spelling, grammar, or mechanics. Your job is to get your ideas down. You will have time to smooth out your writing later.

Name _____ Date _____

Strategies to Get You Started

When you think of the word "draft," think of a work in progress. This stage of the writing process is the time when you form your ideas and sentences into paragraphs. Polishing your work will come later. Decide whether you are going to write by hand or to use a word processor. If you choose to write by hand, gather together several sheets of lined paper and a pencil or pen. If you are using a word processor, be sure to have a disk on which to save your material, and remember to keep any work that you print out, complete with file name. If you do not have a copy of the Chapter 4 Guidelines, ask your instructor for one.

Getting Started

If you have been writing only para-graphs, it is a good idea to consider how a longer piece of writing is developed. The following example follows George and his teacher, Mr. Karachy, through this process. George was asked to write at least two para-graphs about a subject that interested him. After a lot of discussion about possible topics, George decided to write about city noises, but he just couldn't get started. After half an hour of work, he had brainstormed a list of words about city noises:

Examples	people's voices
	cars
	fire alarms
	music
	buses
	ambulance sirens
	the river

That was it. He could see no way to move ahead. He could think of a sentence or two about each, but not how to make the sentences flow together. Mr. Karachy suggested he choose among the following strategies to help him begin. While not magical solutions to the problem, they did give George some direction. These are the strategies Mr. Karachy suggested George use to get started:

1. A story—tell about something that happened to you;

2. A quotation from a magazine, book, or poem;

3. A definition of noise;

4. A description of the kinds of noises you hear;

5. A question for your reader;

6. A statement about your subject.

George reviewed his list of words and realized that he could begin by making a statement.

The city is never quiet.

He realized that when he was younger, he heard the noise as just a blend of many sounds. Now, each sound symbolized some-thing. He went on:

The city is never quiet. When I was young, I didn't understand what all the noises meant. I was never afraid because the noise was just part of life. It was only when I became older that I realized how many of the noises meant trouble.

Writing: A Comprehensive Guide to the Writing Process

Name _____ Date _____

George had found his way to the subject. He was going to write about each of the noises he had listed as part of his brainstorming. Many writers discover their subject as they write. Therefore, just beginning is important. When you are stumped, begin your first paragraph with one of Mr. Karachy's suggestions.

Here is an example of how George could have found quite a different focus by using a quotation from *Familiar Quotations* by John Bartlett. Quotations are organized by subjects in this book, so all George had to do was look under "noise" in the index.

In 1936 Henry Morton said, "The perfect place for a writer is in the hideous roar of a city. . . ." Although Morton may have found noise a help when he wrote, I don't find it helpful at all.

You can see how neatly these sentences introduce the writer's discussion about how bothersome noise is when he has work to do.

George could also have started his paragraph with a combination approach of question and definition. Remember, what you are trying to do with the first sentence is grab the reader's attention.

What is noise? My definition may not be in the dictionary, but it works for me. Noise is bothersome sound that clashes with what I want or need to do.

A question usually engages the reader, who may or may not agree with what is being written—which brings us to another point to consider: What is the writer's purpose? So far, George hasn't considered this. He has been too worried about getting something down on paper. You may find yourself in the same situation when you write, but as you develop your rough draft, your purpose will become clear. You will find you are writing for one of four reasons:

1. You are writing to convince or persuade your reader of something;

2. You are writing to entertain your reader;

3. You are writing to inform your reader;

4. You are writing to describe a scene, person, or event to your reader.

As you may remember, Mr. Karachy also suggested beginning a paragraph with a description.

Example	The buzz of people talking, the high wail of an ambulance, the hum of cars speeding by—these are the noises that form the lullaby of a city child each night.

You now know a number of ways to begin a paragraph. Mr. Karachy's strategies will work to introduce a simple paragraph or to introduce a major report.

Name _____ Date _____

Exercise 4.1

Write an introductory (beginning) sentence for each of the following topics. Use at least three of Mr. Karachy's strategies. This will give you practice using a variety of ways to begin a paragraph.

1. Buses

_____

_____

_____

2. Rivers

_____

_____

_____

3. Friends

_____

_____

_____

4. Mistakes

_____

_____

_____

5. Writing

_____

_____

_____

Name _____ Date _____

The Body of Your Paper

If you are writing more than one paragraph, you need to consider how to move from an introductory paragraph into paragraphs where you give your reader information that supports the idea you introduced in your first paragraph. Let's say that you have written the first paragraph of an essay on city noises. In your first paragraph, you introduce the idea that every noise represents an event of some kind. How can you expand that idea? You can offer facts, names, dates, or ask a series of questions.

Who? _____

What? _____

Where? _____

Why? _____

What does it mean? _____

Examples	Who?	It could be anyone, a friend, a relative, or a stranger.
	What?	ambulance sirens
	Where?	The sound is coming from Main Street.
	Why?	The ambulance drivers are speeding through the streets to get the hurt person to a hospital.
	What does it mean?	It could mean that someone has been badly hurt in an automobile accident. It could mean that a baby is being born.

By answering specific questions, you have discovered usable material.

Review   Before we move on to discuss how to write a conclusion for a series of paragraphs, let's review. We have looked at ways to begin a paragraph:

1. With a story;

2. With a quotation;

3. With a definition;

4. With a description;

5. With a question;

6. With a statement about your subject.

We have discussed how to develop the body of your paper by answering the following questions with specific facts, names, or dates:

1. Who?

2. What?

3. Where?

4. Why?

5. What does it mean?

Now, it's time for some practice!

Writing: A Comprehensive Guide to the Writing Process

Name _____   Date _____

 Exercise 4.2

Write two paragraphs about a friend. Begin by describing how you met and how long you have known each other. Try to write specific details.

Paragraph 1 _____

_____

_____

_____

_____

Now, tell a story about your friend by answering the Who? What? Where? questions.

Paragraph 2 _____

_____

_____

_____

_____

If you want to add further details, continue on the lines that follow, Keep this rough draft in a folder. You may want to polish it later.

_____

_____

_____

Writing: A Comprehensive Guide to the Writing Process

Name _____ Date _____

Writing Your Conclusion

Whether you are writing one paragraph or ten, you are always going to have an introduction, a middle section called "the body," and a conclusion. All of the techniques suggested in this rough draft section can be used any time you write. For example, if you are writing a paragraph answer to a question, you might begin with a quotation, go on to answer the Who, What, When questions, and then write a one-sentence conclusion.

But, what to write in that conclusion? A good piece of writing advice is to return to your beginning paragraph or sentence and restate the idea you started with. Notice how the writer of the following paragraph followed that advice:

For very young children, night noises are just that—noises. Because they have limited experience, they don't realize what the wail of an ambulance can mean. Now that I am older, I have seen accidents and realize that that particular noise can mean someone has been hurt. When I hear an ambulance in the night, I worry about all the people I care about. My baby brother, hearing the same ambulance wail, just continues to drift off to sleep.

Notice that the writer began with a general statement about children and night noises and returned to the idea by writing about a specific child.

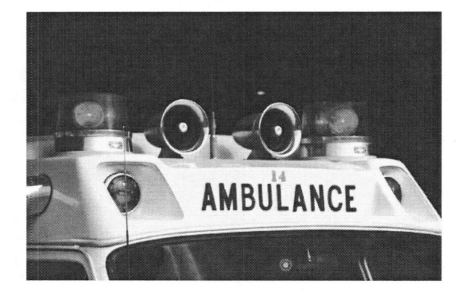

Name _____   Date _____

 Exercise 4.3

Read each of the following paragraphs. Complete them by writing a concluding sentence.

1. Everyone dreams about the perfect vacation, complete with interesting things to do, good food, interesting people, and lots of rest. For some, it might be swimming with dolphins at Disney World. For others, a few days on the beach would be perfect. Friends of mine would probably enjoy flying to a big city to see the sights.

   _____

   _____

2. Can an animal be a person's best friend? Think about it. How many people will wait patiently for hours for you and then greet you with cries of joy? How many people are willing to listen to your every problem? How many people think you are absolutely perfect in every way?

   _____

   _____

3. For once, the house was absolutely quiet. There was no noise except for the drip of the kitchen faucet. Even the traffic outside moved noiselessly by my window. For once, the television wasn't blaring in my ears, the phone wasn't ringing, and my brothers and sisters were nowhere in sight. I was alone.

   _____

   _____

Writing: A Comprehensive Guide to the Writing Process

Name _____   Date _____

Transitional Words

 Transitional words are words that transport or carry the reader smoothly from one sentence or paragraph to the next.

As mentioned before, every piece of writing—no matter how short or how long—must have an introduction, a middle (the "body"), and a conclusion. However, you can't just jump from one to another. If you do, your writing will be choppy and hard to follow. That's where "transitional words" come in. With the help of transitional words, you can move your reader smoothly from one section of your writing to another. Before we look at a list of transitional words, let's look at the word *transition*. Doesn't it remind you of *transportation?* Keeping that in mind will make it easier to remember that transitional words move your reader from place to place. Here are some transitional words and phrases. There are many more.

first	second	later	then	after
front	back	beside	right	left
near	far	over	between	soon
before	during	around	when	as a result
however	rather	nevertheless	below	finally

Some of these transitional words give readers a sense of time or the order in which something should be done. Others help to describe the location of one thing in relationship to another. Others notify the reader that you are going to summarize your thoughts or give an explanation.

 Exercise 4.4

Can you find at least three transitional words or phrases in the paragraphs on this page? List them below, and discuss your answers with a classmate.

_____

_____

_____

_____

_____

_____

Name _____ Date _____

 Exercise 4.5

Underline the transitional words or phrases in each of the following paragraphs.

1. If you want a quick and delicious snack, try one of the new pudding mixes. I don't mean the already-made puddings; I mean the dry pudding mix that needs milk. The first step in making your pudding is to put the dry pudding mix in a bowl. Next, get an eggbeater and two cups of milk. Add the milk to the dry pudding. Now, use the eggbeater to mix the milk and pudding together. After about two minutes, you should have a delicious pudding to eat.

2. As I entered the room, I noticed two large windows directly across from me. In front of the windows was a beautiful maple table on which rested a variety of plants. On the wall to my right, I saw a large painting of a woman holding a child. In the background of the picture, I could see a field of flowers. To my left, I saw another large painting depicting a rose garden. A small sofa was placed in front of each painting. Small, colorful braided rugs were scattered on the hardwood floor. It was a very inviting room.

3. Because we had made our plans early, everything went smoothly. We had called the park early in the day; thus, our picnic site had been reserved for us. Joan drove out an hour before everyone else. As a result, even the food and flowers were arranged when the birthday girl arrived.

Review

When you are writing a rough draft, keep the following in mind:

1. Use a double-spaced format.
2. Save your work.
3. Leave wide margins that allow space to add needed material.
4. Don't worry about correct spelling, grammar, or punctuation—yet!
5. Write a beginning, a middle, and an end to everything, from paragraphs to full reports.
6. Use transitional words to link your paragraphs.
7. Read your material aloud. Check for missing words or confusing sentences.

Writing: A Comprehensive Guide to the Writing Process

Chapter 5: Revising

General Introduction

The good news for students is that this step in the writing process still does not require them to worry about grammar, spelling, and punctuation. That concern will come in the proofreading step. In this step, writers are concerned with rewriting awkward sentences, developing paragraphs in a variety of ways, and adding needed information.

Ideally, of course, you would have the time to sit down with all your students to give them specific revising suggestions. If you have time, great! If not, appoint your own students to be peer editors. In addition to helping other writers, this will give students a chance to sharpen their own critical skills.

Strategies for Revising

There are several strategies you can use. All of them involve having students act as peer editors, both making suggestions and offering encouragement. It's a good idea to mention that part of each editor's job is to make positive statements about the work.

1. Ask students to exchange papers and read for specific types of weaknesses.

2. Have students read their work aloud to another student or to an aide.

3. Divide the class into small groups so that each writer can get feedback from more than one person. This works best if students are given specific tasks. For example, "Juan, you read for confusing sentences. Marie, your job is to be sure the writing contains specific information."

4. Your students can become peer editors for another class. If you decide to do this, students should not put names on their papers. You'll keep the whole process more objective if work is not linked to specific people. Use letters, numbers, or even the names of favorite movie stars for later identification purposes.

It often helps if you write a list of revising suggestions on the board. As your students become more competent peer editors, you can add and/or subtract from this list. Don't be surprised if your first few tries at peer editing are not a smashing success. It takes time and patience. Your students will need to know this too.

Give each of your students a copy of the Revising Checklist. Go over every statement with them. Give them practice using it by having them do the revising activity on page 45. Every problem mentioned on the checklist will be found in this piece of writing. Revision possibilities will be found in the answer key at the end of this book.

(continued)

Chapter 5:
Revising *(continued)*

Meeting Special Needs

Students with special needs should be asked to concentrate on a limited number of revising suggestions. Have them complete the model paragraph with the rest of the class but have them select only two of the suggestions to work on when they do their editing. The Who? What? When? questions are good for them to work with because they are so specific.

If students speak more than one language, ask that they produce their writing in two languages so that they can share it with other bilingual speakers. Bilingual speakers may have a limited vocabulary in their second language. Help them by covering your classroom walls with pictures and words. Encourage them to use the walls as vocabulary prompts.

A Final Word

Remind students that revising can be harder than drafting. Once something is written on paper, it can be very difficult to change. We all feel secure with what we have created and are a little afraid of where change may take us. Vladimir Nabokov, a novelist, once said "I have rewritten—often several times—every word I have ever published." Good writing comes from good rewriting, which is what this step of the writing process is all about.

Name _____ Date _____

Chapter 5: Revising

Revising Checklist

 Revising is the first step in the process of editing. To revise is to rewrite awkward sentences, to write clear topic (introductory) sentences, to add pertinent information, and generally just to smooth out the rough draft.

1. Does each paragraph focus on a specific subject?

2. Has the writer strung many sentences together with "ands" or "buts"? (I call this "anditis disease.")

3. Are any sentences awkward to read or difficult to understand?

4. Has the writer answered the Who? What? When? Where? Why? and How? questions?

5. Can you restate what the writer is trying to say?

6. Is there anything else you would like to know about this subject?

7. What did you find most interesting about this piece of writing?

Name _____ Date _____

 Exercise 5.1

Using your revising checklist as a guide, revise the following paragraph.

A Student's Complaint

My teacher told me that I had to write two paragraphs about something that interested me but she didn't give me any suggestions. How am I supposed to know what to do if nobody tells me what I'm supposed to do and it's her job to tell me what I need to do to get a good grade and she should do it instead of going on and on about lots of other stuff I don't understand. She's the one who is supposed to be the expert in this kind of stuff. How can she expect me to do it if I don't know how or what she wants.

What does she mean by an interest? I do know how to do other things like cards, bikes, and music. All of those things are worth doing and I plan to do them for the rest of my life. I don't know why I have to bother with anything else. Who needs to learn to write about interests?

Name _____   Date _____

The Editor's Job

After you have finished a piece of writing, it is time to move on to a two-step process called editing. When magazine editors revise, they are preparing an article for publication. When you or your classmates edit, you are helping each other to improve work before it is presented to a wider audience—your teacher or others. Any editor's job—whether it be a peer editor or the editor of a magazine or newspaper—is to make the changes needed in written material to make it interesting, readable, and correct.

The editing process is broken down into two specific steps. The first step is to revise—to rewrite awkward sentences, to write clear topic sentences, to add information, and generally just to smooth out what has been written. The second step is to proofread the material, making any spelling, grammar, and punctuation corrections. Since seeing your own mistakes can be difficult, it's a good idea to ask someone else to read over your material. Probably your teacher will team you with a classmate who will become your peer editor. If peer editors do their job at both steps of the editing process, your final draft (your written, revised, corrected, and rewritten work) should be nearly perfect!

Since you will both edit and be edited yourself, you need to know what to look for. Some of the things you need to know about are:

1. topic sentences

2. support for topic sentences

3. ways to develop a paragraph

Let's begin by defining a **topic sentence. It is a sentence that tells your reader what you are going to write about. It is an introduction to a paragraph, a promise to the reader that you are going to discuss a specific subject.** Often, topic sentences are the first sentences in a paragraph, but they can also be located anywhere else in a paragraph. The important thing is that each paragraph has one. When you are revising your written work or editing the work of someone else, be sure topic sentences are included.

Example	Edgar was asked to write a paragraph discussing an activity from which he thought his classmates would benefit. Since Edgar loved fishing, he decided he would write about how much he enjoyed being out in the fresh air. He would also describe how fishing gave him an opportunity to enjoy nature and to relax.

This is what he wrote:

> I love fishing. It is a great way to get outside and enjoy nature firsthand. Outside with nothing but the sounds of birds and water, I get a chance to relax and give myself a break from the daily routine.

On the surface, there doesn't seem to be any problem. Look again. What was the assignment? In his hurry to do his assignment, Edgar forgot his topic. Remember, he was to write about an activity that would benefit his classmates. If you reread the paragraph, you will see that he has not addressed that assignment at all. He needs

Writing: A Comprehensive Guide to the Writing Process

Name _____ Date _____

to write a topic sentence and revise this paragraph to support it. Will this be difficult? No. He just needs to make clear that he recommends fishing for others because it would benefit them. What would you suggest as his topic sentence?

Topic sentence: _____

You probably wrote something like, "Fishing is an activity that benefits young people." If Edgar uses a similar sentence, he will need to make other changes. He can use the same information included in his original paragraph, but he will need to reorganize it to support his topic sentence.

> Many young people would benefit from spending a few hours fishing because it is a restful, relaxing activity. With a fishing rod in hand, the person fishing has nothing to worry about except the joy of being out in the fresh air, enjoying nature.

Notice that the explanation of why fishing is beneficial uses the same example as in the original paragraph, but the writing now has more focus. This paragraph makes clear what the benefits of fishing can be. When you start revising your writing, check to be sure that each paragraph has a clear topic and that the sentences around it are directly linked to that topic.

Now that you understand what a topic sentence is, let's explore further the second issue involved in revising: "Support for Topic Sentences." Every topic sentence needs support. It can't stand alone. It is merely one sentence the role of which is to tell the reader what to expect in a paragraph. By supporting the topic sentence, the writer develops a paragraph. Ways to develop paragraphs are next.

Developing a Paragraph with Examples

A topic sentence introduces your reader to an idea you want to share. It is a promise of sorts. Once you have written a topic sentence, your job in the following sentences is to support it—to supply evidence. Take a minute to look back at the fishing example on page 46 and on this page. When Edgar finally wrote his topic sentence, he told his readers that young people would benefit from fishing. He supported that idea by giving examples of the benefits of fishing. Therefore, one way to support a topic sentence is to give examples. On the line below you will find a topic sentence. Write an example to support that sentence. Think about it. What's good about pizza?

> Pizza is a nourishing snack.

Supporting sentence: _____

Did you have trouble supporting that statement? If you did, think about the beneficial ingredients in pizza—vegetables, cheese, and bread—all ingredients needed in a healthy diet. Here are some steps you can take when trying to find the proof to support a topic sentence:

1. Find the subject of your topic sentence. (In the example above, it was pizza.)

2. List all the words that come to mind when you think about this subject.

Name _____   Date _____

(How about delicious, messy, toma-toes, cheese, fun?)

3. Decide which of these words are directly related to the point you are trying to make. (Only tomatoes and cheese work because you are looking for nourishing ingredients.)

4. Write sentences linking those words to the topic. (Both cheese and tomatoes are part of a healthy diet.)

5. Think of other examples to support your topic sentence and develop your paragraph. (In addition to dairy products and vegetables, pizza is a bread product, and bread is called the "staff of life.")

You get the idea. Be specific. Show your reader exactly what you mean.

Developing a Paragraph with a Story

The second approach to supporting a topic sentence is through a story. Consider the topic sentence about fishing.

> Many young people would benefit from spending a few hours fishing because it is a restful, relaxing activity.

How can this idea be supported with a story? If you have never fished, it would be difficult. But probably Edgar, our fisherman, can think of any number of times he relaxed while fishing:

> Many young people would benefit from spending a few hours fishing because it is a restful, relaxing activity. A couple of years ago, I found myself so stressed out that I couldn't concentrate on my schoolwork. I had papers due, and testing was to begin within a couple of days. Instead of spending all my time studying, I decided to take two hours off to go fishing. Armed with my fishing rod and a bag of sandwiches, I headed for the nearest brook. Before long, the rhythmic sounds of the brook put me to sleep. I woke up a couple hours later, rod in hand, to discover that I was completely rested and ready to go back to my studying. Surely, other young people could benefit from spending some time with a fishing rod and a brook.

Once Edgar got started, he couldn't stop. You will find this happening to you if you write about what you know or what you enjoy. You can't fake ideas in writing. You have to know your subject. If you find that you just can't get started on a piece of writing and that even brainstorming doesn't help, you may simply need to know more about the topic. Do some reading or talk about the subject with a friend. This will help you remember details and focus.

Developing a Paragraph with a Definition

In addition to giving an example or writing an anecdote or story to support or explain a topic sentence, you may choose to give a definition that makes clear to your reader exactly what you are writing about. Going back to the fishing example, we find that Edgar's idea of fishing may not be shared by others. He may need to make it clear to his readers what fishing is for him. For some people, it might be deep-sea fishing on an expensive boat. For others, fishing might be wading in a trout stream, and

Name _____ Date _____

some might think of it as sitting on a dock dangling a rod in the water. Given the evidence in Edgar's writing, we can see that these definitions of fishing are not his, but the following might be:

> Many young people would benefit from spending a few hours fishing because it is a restful, relaxing activity. By fishing I don't mean hiring an expensive boat to zoom over the

water searching for big fish. I mean finding the simplest type of fishing rod possible; grabbing it, something to eat, a few worms, sunglasses, and sunblock; and heading for the quietest brook I can find.

Don't let this work confuse you. Think of revising as developing a work in progress. When you are writing or editing, see if you can use some of these ideas.

Developing a Paragraph with Facts

The fourth way of developing a paragraph to support a topic sentence is by using facts. This strategy requires knowledge of your topic. In Edgar's case, he needed some knowledge of fishing for the paragraph to be credible. His definition made it clear that expensive supplies are not needed to have a good time. Perhaps this fact can be developed to support the topic sentence.

> Many young people would benefit from spending a few hours fishing because it is a restful, relaxing activity. Unlike many sports, fishing does not require a lot of supplies or a lot of money. Of course, anyone who wants the latest equipment can spend a good deal of money at a sporting goods store. But that is not necessary. All that is needed are a rod, a line, a hook, some bait, and a quiet pond or brook. Anyone who wants to take up fishing can find all the necessary information in a book at the local library—

at absolutely no cost. Not having to worry about money or complicated supplies makes fishing a low-key activity.

We have now reviewed four ways of developing a paragraph: through example, anecdote, definition, and facts. Have you found one approach useful for your current writing project? Think about it.

Name _____   Date _____

Comparing and Contrasting

 To *compare* is to look at similarities among items under consideration, while to *contrast* is to show how these things are different.

Developing a Paragraph with Comparison and Contrast

Another approach to developing a paragraph is by comparing and contrasting. Let's start with a different topic sentence.

Example	Not all fast food is junk food.

 Exercise 5.2

Probably the best example of a fast food that isn't a junk food is pizza, so let's compare and contrast it to other fast foods. Remember, when you use comparing and contrasting, you must write both how things are alike and how they are different. Fill in the following chart. This will give you some ideas.

	Pizza	**Other Fast Food**
Similarities	_____ _____ _____	_____ _____ _____
Differences	_____ _____ _____	_____ _____ _____

What kind of ideas did you come up with? Some possible similarities might be that both pizza and other fast foods are fun to eat, taste great, are easy to find, and don't cost too much. As far as differences are concerned, you might have mentioned that pizza offers a wide variety of toppings, including cheese, meat, vegetables, fish, even fruit. Most fast foods don't offer that variety. In addition, many people enjoy pizza for breakfast, as well as for lunch, dinner, or snack time. It is an around-the-clock food. Not only that, pizza can be enjoyed even when eaten cold. Can the same be said of french fries and hamburgers?

You can see that once you start thinking about it, comparing and contrasting is an excellent technique. It just takes some time and thought.

However, there are times when you might want simply to compare two people, subjects, or events. Sometimes, you may wish only to contrast two things. Remember, to compare is to consider similarities. To contrast is to show how things are different. Both are valid ways to develop a topic sentence and paragraph.

Writing: A Comprehensive Guide to the Writing Process

Name _____ Date _____

Exercise 5.3

Put together a paragraph comparing and contrasting pizza with other fast foods. You may base the paragraph on the ideas mentioned on page 48 and page 50 as well as your own. Good luck!

_____

_____

_____

_____

Exercise 5.4

Read the following paragraph. How did the writer develop the topic sentence? Did the writer use examples, stories, definitions, facts, comparisons, contrasts?

Saturdays

There are basically two kinds of Saturdays. First is the work Saturday. You know that kind. It happens when you have put off completing a paper that is due, or when you have to do something about the mess in your room. A work Saturday also happens when the family decides it is time to visit Great Aunt Helen. On a work Saturday you wake up knowing that your time is not your own. Although work Saturdays are necessary, free Saturdays are usually a lot more fun. On a free Saturday you wake up and realize there is absolutely nothing you have to do. The next few hours are yours, all yours. You can decide to sleep in, visit a friend, prepare a big breakfast, take a drive, go shopping, or just relax. It is up to you. Given the choice, I think most of us would choose free Saturdays. How about you?

1. What is the subject of this paragraph? _____

_____

2. What is the writer's attitude toward Saturdays? _____

_____

3. How does the writer show the differences between the Saturdays? _____

_____

4. Does the writer show how Saturdays are similar? _____

5. Identify the type of paragraph development the writer used. _____

_____

Name _____   Date _____

Exercise 5.5

Now it is your chance to write. Use the subject of Saturday. You may develop your paragraph however you wish, but you must identify the type of development used. Remember, the possibilities are example, anecdote, definition, facts, comparison, contrast. Good luck.

_____

_____

_____

_____

_____

_____

_____

_____

_____

_____

Writing: A Comprehensive Guide to the Writing Process

Name _____ Date _____

Titles

The last issue is really what is first in any story—the title. Most people check the title of a written work before they decide whether or not to read it. Your job as a writer is to develop a title that will encourage your reader's interest.

It is a good idea to start thinking about a title as you begin your rough draft. This does not commit you to that title. It merely means that you have a "working title," a place to begin. As you develop your paper, you may find the focus of the paper changing, and this change should be reflected in your title.

There are at least three kinds of titles to choose from. The easiest is the direct title stating exactly what you are writing about. For example, if you are presenting a brief history of one of the battles of World War II, you might use a title such as "Pearl Harbor" or "Midway." If you are writing about a person, that person's name might do. If you are writing about a movie, the title of the movie could easily become your title. Granted, this type of title isn't particularly interesting, and it does not show much creativity on the part of the writer. But it does make clear the intent of the writing. This type of title is best used for serious work.

Headline

 The headline is a form of title indicating the subject matter of the writing that follows it. Headlines are usually written in an attention-grabbing manner. Common places to find headlines are in newspapers and magazines.

A second title type is one that suggests the subject of the writing in such a way that the reader is anxious to investigate. If you look at newspaper and magazine headlines, you will find that headlines are written in this way—for example, "500 Jobs Lost," "Danger in Your Neighborhood," "Bus Riders Beware, Trouble Ahead." The headline, similar to a title, is written to capture attention.

Name _____ Date _____

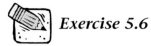 *Exercise 5.6*

Headline Hunting

Take a few minutes to go headline hunting through current newspapers and magazines. On the lines below, list the headlines that caught your attention. Notice the characteristics of a good headline. Working with other people's titles will help you to decide on better titles for your own work. When you have finished, discuss your findings with a classmate.

Notable Headlines

_____

_____

_____

_____

_____

_____

Can you see any similarities among the noteworthy headlines? List them below.

_____

_____

_____

Good headlines usually feature active verbs. They also rely on the use of easily recognized names or nicknames. For example, how often have you read about The Big Apple rather than about New York? Including a familiar word or name in a title is a good way to get attention. Can you find an example of this type of headline?

_____

_____

Writing: A Comprehensive Guide to the Writing Process

Name _____   Date _____

More on Titles

I'll bet you never realized how much there is to say about titles. We've talked about two kinds of titles: the straightforward-no-fooling around type and the action title loaded with memorable names or action words. Before you read on, check the sports page and notice the type of headlines used there. You'll find some serious, but a lot of "playful," titles (no pun intended). Some playful titles use alliterative words, that is, words that begin with the same initial letters.

| **Examples** | Feisty Football Team Fends off Foes |
| | Talented Team Trounces Tigers |

People enjoy this type of title, just as they enjoy rhymes of all kinds. That brings us to another type of title: one that is playful and rhymes. You might entitle a paper on astronomy, for example, "All Eyes Are on the Skies." Equally effective is taking a well-known expression and twisting is to suit the focus of your writing. For example, a paper about the difficulties of getting up in the morning might be entitled "The Early Bird May Get the Worm, But Who Wants It?"

As you can see, the possibilities are endless. Just be sure that your title matches the tone of your writing. You do not want a "cute" title when your paper has a serious message. Make a point of noticing titles of books, magazines, and articles. Compare the title with the article. Why did the writer select the title? It might be interesting to keep a record of what you find. This record may also be helpful when you are trying to write titles of your own.

Name _____ Date _____

 Exercise 5.7

Give each of the paragraphs below an effective title.

1. Two men lost in the woods for ten days were found yesterday camped out in an old hunting lodge. Although they had not carried food supplies with them, they were able to live on what they could find in the woods. Both men were from Los Angeles and had little wilderness experience. One commented, "We just did what we had to do to live."

   Title _____

2. Sylvia Bracus was named "Classic Cook of the Year" by a panel of judges meeting in New York City. Bracus, whose specialty is cabbage rolls, admitted that she had trained hard for the competition. "I was up before 6 A.M. every morning perfecting my cabbage rolls. My family learned to love them for breakfast."

   Title _____

3. Local sports fans were thrilled by the performance of senior Hitty Winn at last night's basketball battle against the Winthrop High School team. Winn couldn't miss. All but four of her shots were bull's-eyes. Her opponents could do nothing to stop her.

   Title _____

4. A small child who wandered away from home yesterday afternoon was found safe and sound in his own backyard. Of course, his backyard consists of 85 acres of woodlands. When asked why he had left the fenced area behind his house, he said, "I wanted to see the world."

   Title _____

Chapter 6: Proofreading

General Introduction

Proofreading is the fifth step of the writing process. If you and your students have done these lessons sequentially, you have guided them through brainstorming, sentence development, rough draft writing, and revising. During the proofreading step, the writer looks for errors in usage, mechanics, and spelling. Of course, computer checks will take care of many of these problems, but not all. It is up to your students and their peer editors to take the major responsibility.

Strategies for Proofreading

With so much to consider when correcting for grammar and spelling, many students may be overwhelmed if asked to be responsible for all possible errors in their writing. One way to handle this is by helping students to develop individual checklists itemizing the kinds of errors they most frequently make. To start, you might develop a class checklist listing the errors you see on many papers. An example of a beginning-of-the-year list appears on page 59.

The advantage of beginning with a class checklist is that everyone can correct for these errors and, by discussing them, actually teach each other. As students master items on their checklists, they can cross them off and add new items.

Checklists facilitate successful peer proofreading because they allow focus on specifics. During a proofreading session, divide the class into groups of two or three. Each paper to be evaluated must be accompanied by a checklist. If checklist items are numbered, peer editors can simply write the appropriate number next to a problem in the paper. Then the student responsible for the error makes the correction.

Meeting Special Needs

To make it easier for students to deal with checklists, try dividing the checklist into three sections, with only a couple of items in each section. For the spelling checklist, have students write down troublesome words.

Format Checklist

1. Have I double-spaced my material?

2. Have I included a title?

Grammar and Mechanics Checklist

1. Have I capitalized the first word of every sentence?

2. Does every sentence have a subject and a verb?

Spelling Checklist

1. *A lot* is two words.

2. *There* means a place.

3. *Their* shows ownership.

(continued)

Chapter 6:
Proofreading *(continued)*

A Final Word

Some students find this step one of the least enjoyable parts of writing. It requires attention to what can sometimes seem like trivial details. Peer editing can help make it less tedious. Good proofreading exercises can be useful. But your enthusiasm about the importance of this step can be the greatest motivator of all.

Name _____ Date _____

Chapter 6: Proofreading

Proofreading Checklist

 Proofreading is the second step in the editing process. It is the act of carefully checking the revised draft for errors in usage, grammar, punctuation, and spelling and correcting any mistakes found.

1. Do all my sentences end with a period, question mark, or exclamation point?

2. Can I find a verb and subject in each of my sentences?

3. Do the subject and verb agree, singular subject, singular verb, etc.?

4. Have I used so many *ands* that I will be accused of having "anditis"?

5. Have I used *a lot* as two words?

6. Have I used spell check or looked up unfamiliar words in the dictionary?

7. Are all proper nouns capitalized?

8. Have I separated words in a series with commas?

9. Have I used *there, their, they're* correctly? (The computer can't help here.)

10. Have I used *your* and *you're* correctly?

Name _____   Date _____

Looking for Nitty-Gritty Errors

At last, you get a chance to look for those spelling, grammar, and other mechanical errors you have been worried about. Up until this point, you have been concerned with content and the arrangement of words, sentences, and paragraphs. Now, you are going to look for the nitty-gritty errors. As in the revising step, having someone else proofread your work is a good idea. To make your proofreader's job easier, put together a checklist to accompany your rough draft. This will give your reader some direction. Don't think that because you have a proofreader, you are not responsible for checking your own work. A careful writer will always double-check.

If you are using a computer, depending on the spell check and grammar check is not enough. Although these checks do a wonderful job, they cannot recognize that a correctly spelled word is inappropriate in a given sentence. For example, a spell check would accept the following: "President Eisenhower did a good joy during World War II." The computer would be perfectly happy with the word *joy*, although it makes no sense in this sentence.

Your teacher may help your class develop a checklist, or you may be asked to develop one on your own. To help you do so, three proofreading exercises follow. Do the work and check your answers. The types of errors you make will help identify the suggestions that should appear on your checklist.

Writing: A Comprehensive Guide to the Writing Process

Name _____ Date _____

 Exercise 6.1

Read the following paragraph carefully. Circle any errors and make the necessary corrections on the appropriate lines below. When you have completed the page, check your answers.

Beautiful People

1.   When you hear the expression "beautiful people," what due you think about? Do you

2. think about a famous movie actor or actress, a rock star, a millionaire—what comes to mine?

3. Most people use the express to indicate someone who is well know and very attractive. I wish

4. we could define it in another way that wood recognize that beauty is more then what is seen

5. on the outside. Let us face it. Everyone can't be beautiful and wealthy. A lot of us appear to

6. be both pour and ordinary in appearance. In spite of this, we all have the opportunity to

7. accomplish some good in our lives and thus deserve as much recognition and admiration as

8. those who have "beautiful" exteriors.

Corrections

Line 1   _____   Line 5   _____

Line 2   _____   Line 6   _____

Line 3   _____   Line 7   _____

Line 4   _____   Line 8   _____

     Writing: A Comprehensive Guide to the Writing Process

Name _____ Date _____

 Exercise 6.2

Read the following paragraph carefully. Circle any errors and make the necessary corrections on the lines on the next page. When you have completed this exercise, check your answers.

Remembering Miss Otis

1. Miss Otis lived opposite my family on West street. I frequently say her in her garden down

2. on her hands and knees attacking the weeds that had dared to grow up around her "darling

3. plants." I write "darling plants" because that is what she called them. Each petunia pansy and

4. daisy was an individual to Miss Otis. She tended them as she would have beloved children.

5. Miss Otis dressed in an unconventional manner. Her skirts were long and usually of a very

6. flimsy, almost transparent material. She always wore a quantity of necklaces, bracelets and

7. rings. Although her worn face suggested age, she bravely wore her hair long and curly. She

8. never appeared without complete makeup, which included false eye lashes and crimson

9. lipstick. In addition she always wore a large floppy hat bedecked with colorful plastic flowers.

10. Growing up, I always though of her as being very strange. Why did she dress so? Why the

11. heavy makeup. Why couldn't she see that many people made fun of her? I never found

12. out the answer to these questions. Although I have forgotten much of my childhood, I'll

13. never forget Miss Otis.

(continued)

Writing: A Comprehensive Guide to the Writing Process

Name _____   Date _____

Corrections

Line 1 _____   Line 8 _____

Line 2 _____   Line 9 _____

Line 3 _____   Line 10 _____

Line 4 _____   Line 11 _____

Line 5 _____   Line 12 _____

Line 6 _____   Line 13 _____

Line 7 _____

Writing: A Comprehensive Guide to the Writing Process

Name _____ Date _____

 Exercise 6.3

Read the following paragraph carefully. Circle any errors and make the necessary corrections. When you have completed this page, check your answers.

Blue and Other Colorful Words

1. Have you ever had the Monday morning blues? Have you ever wondered why feeling

2. sad is described as "blue"? When you stop to think about it blue is what we all look for

3. when we look up at the sky. It is gray days that makes us feel sad. Why did "blue" get

4. stuck with such a bad repetition. Why do we so often use color to describe situations. Is

5. our language full of colorful words because everyone can relate to color? Who knows?

6. No matter what the reason is, English is colorful. A jealous person is "green" with envy.

7. If people are furious we say they are seeing "red." We turn "white" with fear and

8. "purple" with passion. A thief can be caught "red-handed" and a talented gardener has a

9. "green thumb." Color helps to make our language vivid.

Corrections

Line 1 _____   Line 6 _____

Line 2 _____   Line 7 _____

Line 3 _____   Line 8 _____

Line 4 _____   Line 9 _____

Line 5 _____

Writing: A Comprehensive Guide to the Writing Process

Chapter 7: The Final Draft

General Introduction

Writing a final draft is a step of the writing process your students have been anticipating since the day they worked on brainstorming techniques. This last step is just a matter of asking students to write a draft ready for evaluation and publishing.

Final Draft Strategies

I've found that the mention of "publishing" is the best motivator for reluctant writers. If student writers understand that their writing is going to move beyond the teacher's desk, their work takes on increased importance.

There are a variety of ways to publish student work. One is to print student work in a class newspaper, which can be distributed throughout your school. If you decide to do this, you may want to ask students to experiment with a variety of formats. For example, you might ask that certain students be responsible for a "Letters to the Editor" section, where they can write about issues of interest to other students, such as sports, fashion, school problems, curfews, etc. Other students might enjoy writing short stories, essays, local news, or advertisements. Suggestions for all of these can be found in Part III of this book.

Another publishing avenue is having your students contribute to the local newspaper. The public is showing a great deal of interest in the young people of today, and your local newspaper might be willing to publish a weekly or biweekly column written by young people. Another possibility is asking students to respond to articles they have read in magazines or newspapers. It is a rare publication that does not have a "Letters to the Editor" page.

In addition, magazines designed for youth sponsor dozens of writing contests. Teacher magazines are another source of information about writing contests. Of course, the Internet is filled with writing opportunities. It is just a matter of finding the time to access this marvelous tool. If you don't have the time, ask one of your students to do the necessary research. No one said you had to do everything, although some days it seems like it.

If possible, all students should have writing folders where final drafts are kept. Be sure to ask for a date on each final draft. In that way, your students will have a record of the progress they have made through their work with you. Journals, which are discussed in Part III, are another way for students to document their progress.

Meeting Special Needs

Some students may have difficulty accepting the need for more than one draft. Stress the fact that a rough draft is a temporary draft; a final draft is the real thing—it's finished. If you can, make a second copy of some final drafts to be taken home and read to families. Bilingual families can actually learn from their students' work. It's another way to bring school and home together.

(continued)

Chapter 7:
The Final Draft *(continued)*

A Final Word

The following student page suggests publishing guidelines for your students to consider. Even though many of them will not be interested in having their work published, they may be interested in just how much work goes into that process. No specific exercises have been provided for this chapter. However, you may certainly ask students either to prepare a final draft of work already in their writing folder or to complete one of the ideas suggested in the strategies section of this chapter.

Chapter 7: The Final Draft

Final Draft

 The final draft of a manuscript incorporates all the changes and corrections made in the editing process. It is the final product of the writing process.

The final draft is the last step of the writing process, the product you will turn in to your teacher for evaluation and, possibly, publication. It should be done in your best handwriting or on the computer. The question is, Where to publish? There are lots of possibilities, including classroom newspapers, bulletin boards, local newspapers, magazines, home pages, and, of course, your writing folder or portfolio.

Even if you are not interested in submitting your material to a magazine or newspaper, you may be interested to know how it is done. The following guidelines will help you plan your entry into the publishing world if and when you are ready.

General Publishing Guidelines

1. Read several issues of the magazine or newspaper in which you are interested.

2. Look for author guidelines. Frequently these will be found near the credits. Newspapers usually publish them on the editorial page. Some magazines have specific guidelines to send to those who request them. There is no harm in asking.

3. Do monthly issues of the magazine have themes—that is, are all the articles in an issue related in some way? If so, your writing will have to relate to a specific theme.

4. If you have guidelines, follow them exactly. Otherwise, the material will not be considered for publication.

5. Most publications require the following:

   (a) A self-addressed stamped envelope

   (b) Multiple copies of the material

   (c) Single submissions, meaning that you submit your material to no one else until after it has been accepted or rejected by the magazine in question

   (d) A cover letter stating your reasons for submitting your writing to this publication

   (e) A disk (Be sure that you have both a personal disk and one to mail out.)

Part II:
Audience and Purpose

General Introduction

Students don't always understand that different situations require different language and behavior. What may be appropriate for a group of teenagers discussing the latest music may not be appropriate for a conversation with their grandparents. This holds true in writing. The newest styles can be called "hot" in a review for the school newspaper, but for parents they should be "fashionable."

As well as considering the audience, writers must also keep in mind the purpose of their writing. Do they wish to persuade, inform, entertain, or describe? Although each type of writing shares characteristics with the others, each has characteristics writers can use to their advantage as they write. For example, persuasive writing will include emotionally charged words, informative writing will emphasize facts, while passages written to entertain will contain all of those elements and more.

Strategies

Discussing appropriate language with teenagers can be a hair-raising experience for anyone. Sometimes, the words that issue from "the mouths of babes" stop us in our tracks. No matter what the dangers are, young writers must learn that if they wish to be heard, they must consider their audience. Asking writers to write the same message for two or three audiences is a good way of making this point. Possible subjects are a favorite rock group, a weekend party, a driving experience, or even a meal. Ask that they start by writing a dialogue between friends. Then, ask that the same content be written as it would be first for parents and finally for a group of strangers.

To help students understand both audience and purpose, ask them to do at least one of the activities suggested in this unit. The slang activity will help student writers understand that each generation has its own slang terms, which may or may not be understood by other generations. The magazine activity will help them to understand how periodicals adapt their material to specific interest and age groups through content and language. Through this activity students will also learn how purpose determines both content and language. To prepare for the magazine activity, collect materials published for a variety of age groups. Students who have difficulty in reading the more sophisticated magazines can benefit from working with magazines designed for children. This activity can be modified to be used with catalogs, since catalogs for companies such as L.L. Bean are designed for specific audiences. The Bean outdoors catalog, for example, is published for everyone who enjoys outdoors activities, from backpacking to fishing.

(continued)

Part II:
Audience and Purpose *(continued)*

Meeting Special Needs

Bilingual students can take this opportunity to write at least one of their messages in a language other than English. This should help nurture the idea that being bilingual is a tremendous advantage. To offer your support, encourage your bilingual students to read their written work in both English and their second language. You may find other students anxious to learn some words in another language. In another situation, you may want to ask a student to use ASL (American Sign Language) in order to share what he/she has written.

A Final Word

Of course, it is pointless to consider purpose and audience early in the year, when students are trying just to get their pens and computer keys in motion. It is better to work on the steps of the writing process first, progressing to audience and purpose after writers are feeling secure in their ability to find something to say.

Audience and Purpose

The Reading Audience

If you usually think of an audience as a group of people listening to music or watching a performance, you need to broaden your definition a bit. Every time you put words on paper, you are writing for an audience—the audience that is going to read and respond to your words. Just as performers gear their performances to their audiences, you as a writer must do the same if you want your words to be read.

To keep your reading audience happy, you must first select material of interest to them. You then must be sure to use the type of language they respond to. If you speak two languages, you obviously will select the language your audience understands. You also need to consider the type of language you use. All languages include both formal and informal components. When speaking or writing informally, you don't need to worry about grammar and mechanics as much as you should in more formal settings. Most of the writing you do for school exemplifies formal writing. Slang is appropriate in informal situations when you and your friends are hanging out.

Slang

 Slang is very informal language, often quite colorful, that is usually relatively specific to a certain time, place, and group of people.

Developing a dictionary of slang terms can be an interesting way to compare the slang terms of today with those of the past. To do this activity, you will need to interview people from different generations, like your thirty-something neighbor, your mother, and your grandmother. Don't just think "old." Language is constantly changing, and the slang terms you use may be quite different from those your older brothers and sisters used. To prove that point, do the following activity.

Name _____   Date _____

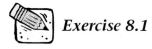 *Exercise 8.1*

Slang Through the Ages

Listed below are slang terms from the past with their definitions. Next to each, write an example of today's slang with a similar meaning. When you have finished, check with other "audiences" to discover if they can define either the past slang or the current slang.

Past Slang	Meaning	Current Slang
tootsie wootsie	girlfriend or boyfriend	_____
swish	stylish, fashionable	_____
swinging	dancing	_____
living it up	having a good time	_____
my old flame	a romance from the past	_____
playing with fire	dangerous actions	_____
a lotta oomph	lively	_____
small fry	young kids	_____
terrific	excellent	_____
to spoon	to get romantic	_____
awesome	terrific	_____
groovy	wonderful	_____
with it	moving with the times	_____
the cat's pajamas	terrific	_____
swell	very good	_____
soapy	overdone	_____
down and out	having a difficult time	_____

Compare your lists with those of others. If possible, combine the lists to create a dictionary of slang through the ages. Keeping in mind how quickly slang terms change, why do you think it isn't a good idea to use slang in formal writing?

Writing: A Comprehensive Guide to the Writing Process

Name _____   Date _____

Understanding Audience and Purpose

Newspapers and magazines are published to make money. Therefore, their editors, publishers, and writers are careful to select material that will interest a specific audience. As you know, magazines like *Car and Driver* appeal to car fanatics. *Seventeen* is a magazine for teenaged girls. *Golf Digest* probably will not appeal to anyone who does not play golf. Newspapers are written for a much broader audience. If you look through a newspaper, you will find something for everyone. There are editorials and news articles for those interested in local and national concerns, comics for both kids and adults, crossword puzzles for word lovers, and advertisements for everyone.

Just as newspaper and magazine writers must be concerned with their audience, you, as a writer, must be too. Not only should you choose language that your audience can understand, but you should also decide what you are trying to do with your writing. Are you trying to persuade your audience to adopt a particular point of view? Do you hope to entertain? Or is your purpose to inform? Each of these purposes places different responsibilities on the writer.

(continued)

Writing: A Comprehensive Guide to the Writing Process

Name _____   Date _____

Persuasive Writing

Persuasive writing is designed to convince its audience of something.

Good writers immediately make clear to their readers what they believe.

Examples	Speed limits should be lowered.
	School uniforms solve many school problems.
	Everyone should know two languages.
	Ice cream is good for everyone.

No matter what the thesis (what the writer is trying to prove), the writer must provide evidence to support that thesis. This can be done with facts, examples, statistics, or stories. Just as a detective needs evidence to prove the solution to a crime, you need evidence to convince your reader that you know what you are talking about.

Exercise 8.2

Choose one of the statements in the Examples box above. List as many ideas as you can to support the statement.

_____

_____

_____

_____

_____

_____

_____

_____

_____

_____

_____

_____

Name _____ Date _____

Narrative

 A narrative is a story or the retelling of a sequence of events, either real or fictional.

Narrative writing is written to entertain. It usually presents a series of events, which may be funny, sad, scary. This type of writing is a little less formal than persuasive writing. It frequently contains characters, descriptions, and dialogue.

To know my Aunt Sadie was to love her. She didn't have a mean bone in her body. One of her favorite expressions was "For land's sake, child, sit yourself down and eat a little something." Those "somethings" were

delicious little dumplings stuffed with savory meat, turnovers filled with jam, slices of her famous spice cake—there was always something waiting for me. That is, until Aunt Sadie's ninetieth birthday.

I knew when I entered the kitchen that something was wrong. Instead of standing at the sink or by the stove, Aunt Sadie was sitting in a chair. Without being asked, she explained, "It's time someone cooked for me."

 Exercise 8.3

Think of an event you saw recently, or an experience you had. Write down the sequence of the event or experience.

Examples	1. I overslept.
	2. I missed the bus.
	3. I had to walk to school.

1. _____

2. _____

3. _____

4. _____

5. _____

6. _____

        Writing: A Comprehensive Guide to the Writing Process

Name _____   Date _____

Descriptive Writing

Descriptive writing is writing that appeals to one or more of the five senses: hearing, sight, smell, touch, and taste.

This type of writing relies heavily on specific nouns, verbs, and adjectives.

Examples	The comforting crackling of the fire lulled me to sleep.
	As I entered the kitchen, I spied a plate of golden-brown fried chicken.
	A spicy fragrance filled the room.
	The roughness of the material reddens my chapped hands.
	The springtime sweetness of maple syrup will linger on my lips.

Exercise 8.4

List as many words as you can that appeal to each of the five senses.

Sight

_____

_____

_____

_____

Sound

_____

_____

_____

_____

Smell

_____

_____

_____

Taste

_____

_____

_____

Touch

_____

_____

_____

_____

Writing: A Comprehensive Guide to the Writing Process

Name _____   Date _____

Informative Writing

 Informative writing, sometimes called expository, is written to provide information.

A good deal of your classroom writing is informative. If your social studies teacher asks for an essay on a World War II battle, he/she wants facts. Emotional words, tedious descriptions, and inaccurate information have no place in informative writing. A famous television character of the 1960s used to say "Just the facts, ma'am, just the facts." Keep those facts in mind when you are writing to inform.

 Exercise 8.5

Rewrite each sentence below to be informative, not descriptive, persuasive, or emotional.

1. The cunning mouse taunted the cat, darting nimbly past it as the feline stretched sleepily by the fire.

   _____

   _____

2. World War I started around the beginning of the twentieth century.

   _____

   _____

3. Our football team, which is absolutely the best team in the whole state, lost about half of its games this season, but it wasn't their fault.

   _____

   _____

4. In order to make photocopies whose velvety blacks and flawless whites suggest fine photographs, start by pulling the drawer thingy out and putting paper in it.

   _____

   _____

5. Colombia is the biggest country in North America. _____

   _____

Writing: A Comprehensive Guide to the Writing Process

Name _____ Date _____

 Exercise 8.6

Now that you have an idea of the different purposes for writing, use this information to evaluate a magazine or catalog. The questions below will guide you through this evaluation.

As you know, careful writers write for specific audiences and for specific purposes. In this exercise you are to determine both the audience and the purpose of a magazine or catalog. Your first step, of course, is to select a magazine.

1. Title of publication: _____

2. Describe the cover. _____

3. Would this cover appeal to all age groups? _____ Why? Why not? _____
   _____

4. Consider the words of the title. What does the title suggest—self-improvement, general information, sports, fashion, something else?
   _____

5. In order to be successful, magazines must attract readers and advertisers. The advertisements appearing in a magazine indicate the market on which the magazine focuses. Clothing stores and fashion designers are going to concentrate their ads in fashion magazines. Read through several advertisements in the magazine you are evaluating. What do they have in common?
   _____
   _____

6. Read at least one article. What is the point the writer is trying to make? If the article is well written, the purpose should be clear within a paragraph or two. Indicators of purpose are word choice, use of facts to support ideas, emotional words, and dialogue. If you are not sure, refer to the chart of writing purposes on the following page. Be sure you can defend your choice.
   _____
   _____

7. Based on your answers, describe the intended audience for this magazine. Explain your reasons.
   _____
   _____

8. Under what circumstances do you need to consider the audience and purpose of your writing? _____
   _____

Writing: A Comprehensive Guide to the Writing Process

Name _____   Date _____

Blending the Purposes

In many types of writing, a variety of approaches is needed to convey your message. If you read through some letters to the editor in your newspaper, for example, you will find that the writers may want to pass along information on a subject as well as promote a point of view.

The following chart summarizes the purposes for writing and the characteristics of each type. Remember, any piece of writing may contain elements of persuasive, narrative, and informative writing.

Purposes for Writing	Characteristics
To persuade (Persuasive Writing)	Emotional language Definite ideas
To entertain (Narrative Writing)	A series of events (storyline) Characters Dialogue and descriptions
To inform (Informative Writing)	Presentation of facts Usually formal language

Writing: A Comprehensive Guide to the Writing Process

Name _____   Date _____

 Exercise 8.7

Read the following letter to the editor. Then, using the chart on page 79, answer the questions below.

Dear Editor:

After reading your editorial of April 18, I am convinced that many Americans do not realize that Patriots' Day is celebrated in remembrance of the first battle of the Revolutionary War. Why do many of my generation remember? We remember because we were taught a poem that locked the date in our minds. If the public schools of today would follow the traditions established in the one-room schoolhouses of the past, every child in America would know both the significance of Patriots' Day and the Henry Wadsworth Longfellow poem that would lock this event in their memories.

 Listen, my children, and you shall hear
Of the midnight ride of Paul Revere,
On the eighteenth of April, in Seventy Five;
Hardly a man is now alive
Who remembers that famous day and year. . . .

This type of poetry makes history memorable. Let's get back to the tradition of expecting students to think and remember. It is time for the schools of America to return to some of the educational practices of the past.

A Concerned Citizen

Name _____ Date _____

1. Are there any elements of informative writing in this letter? If so, list those elements below.

   _____

   _____

   _____

   _____

2. Are there any elements of persuasive writing in this letter? If so, list those elements below.

   _____

   _____

   _____

   _____

3. Are there any elements of narrative writing in this letter? If so, list those elements below.

   _____

   _____

   _____

   _____

4. Can you support the statement that this letter exemplifies any one of the three purposes of writing? Support your answer.

   _____

   _____

   _____

   _____

5. What audience is the writer trying to reach? _____

   _____

Writing: A Comprehensive Guide to the Writing Process

Part III:
Exploring the Writing World

General Introduction

As teachers, we engage in writing daily. We write notes to parents, reports for administrators, e-mail to friends, comments on student papers, minutes of meetings, etc. We feel comfortable about our writing skills because we practice them. Even so, I find that sitting down in front of my computer after several days away from any writing tasks is pure misery. I can't seem to organize my thoughts. The words don't come. The screen remains blank for what seems like hours. If this is true for you, also consider what this means for your students. The message is clear: Students need regular writing practice if they are to be proficient at expressing their thoughts.

Strategies

Not all students are going to write essays with ease. Therefore, offering students a variety of ways to express their thoughts is essential for them to develop any writing confidence. In this unit are descriptions of a variety of writing assignments that should challenge and interest your students.

Meeting Special Needs

If your ESL students have difficulties completing an assignment in English, ask that they write their thoughts in their first language and then translate the material into English. Many bilingual speakers regularly think in their first language and then translate into English.

A Final Word

Begin each of these assignments with your students by asking them to brainstorm, develop sentences, and write a rough draft. If a final draft is needed, have them continue with revising, proofreading, and writing a final draft.

Name _____ Date _____

Exploring the Writing World

Writing Essays

Essay

 An essay is a group of paragraphs supporting a thesis statement (a clear statement of the subject to be explored). Essays are usually written in a formal style.

What is an essay? Does writing one sound difficult to do? Actually, the word *essay* can mean "an attempt or experiment." When used as a writing term, it refers to a group of paragraphs relating to one subject. If using the first definition helps you to understand what an essay is, think of it as an attempt to expose or explore a subject.

The structure of an essay is similar to that of a good paragraph. Think of a paragraph as a mini-essay, with an introduction (the topic sentence), body, and a conclusion. An essay has the same structure. It

begins with an introduction and continues with a topic sentence stating the thesis. This thesis is then supported through definition, example, anecdote, facts, or by comparing and contrasting. Finally, an essay ends with a summary paragraph that returns the reader to the thesis. If you can write a paragraph, you can write an essay.

Begin your essay by brainstorming. Develop a tight structure or form for your essay. In this type of assignment, as in any assignment longer than a paragraph or two, it is a good plan to set up a simple, informal outline.

Outline

 An outline is a graphic way to structure your ideas. It lists main points as major headings and supporting materials as subheads under the appropriate major headings.

Let's say you have been asked to write an informal essay on the advantages of being bilingual. The outline for this essay could look like this:

Thesis: Bilingual speakers have many advantages over people who speak only one language.

I. Introductory paragraph including thesis statement

II. Supporting paragraphs

  A. Mention one advantage

    1. An example of the advantage

    2. Transitional sentence to next paragraph

  B. Mention a second advantage

    1. An anecdote to illustrate advantage

    2. Transitional sentence to next paragraph

  C. Mention a third advantage

    1. Facts to support this advantage

Name _____ Date _____

> 2. Transitional sentence to next paragraph
> III. Summarizing Paragraph
>> A. Refer to advantages
>> B. Restate thesis

If you have developed a list of words during a brainstorming session, the next step is figuring out how to put these words first into sentences and then into paragraphs. The outline helps you to organize your ideas. Remember, if you decide to quote or paraphrase material from someone else's writing, you must give credit to that person. Ask your teacher to explain how to do this.

 Exercise 9.1

Outlining Practice 1

In this exercise you will be working with a list brainstormed from the words "city noises."

Examples	voices	cars	buses
	fire alarms	ambulance sirens	music

Let's expand that list to include other noises:

Examples	footsteps	airplanes	machine noises
	people noises	police whistles	

The task is to organize these words into a logical sequence by selecting major points. First, you need to decide how you are going to introduce your subject. What are you going to say about "city noises?" Here are some possibilities:

1. You might state that there are many types of noises.
2. You might state that the city is never quiet.
3. You might even say that the noises are comforting.
4. You might think of a totally different possibility!

The statement you select will be called your **thesis**. Your thesis tells your reader what you are going to write about. Write your thesis on the following line.

Thesis: _____

Name _____ Date _____

The next step is to select major categories of information to support your thesis. If you look at the brainstorming list, you will find that all the noises can fit under one or two categories: people noises and machine noises. These will become I and II under your thesis statement.

I. _____

II. _____

To complete your outline, list the other brainstorming words under one of these two categories. Do this by filling in the slots below. Notice the space for a title.

Title _____

Thesis: _____

I. _____

    A. _____

    B. _____

    C. _____

    D. _____

II. _____

    A. _____

    B. _____

    C. _____

    D. _____

    E. _____

Name _____ Date _____

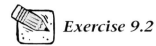 *Exercise 9.2*

Outlining Practice 2

Outlining is simply a way of organizing your thoughts before you begin a writing project. Almost anything can be broken down into categories. For example, think of preparing a meal. Your first step is to decide what you want to eat; next, you purchase the food; and finally, you prepare the food for consumption. To outline this process, you would assign Roman numerals to the major points and list words under these that would help you develop those ideas.

Examine the list of words below. Then, organize these words into an outline. Notice that there are two major categories.

aerobics	radio	swimming
television	couch potatoes	running
magazines	sitting	biking
walking	stretching	
movies	active people	

Title _____

Thesis: _____

I. _____

   A. _____

   B. _____

   C. _____

   D. _____

II. _____

   A. _____

   B. _____

   C. _____

   D. _____

Writing: A Comprehensive Guide to the Writing Process

Name _____ Date _____

 Exercise 9.3

Respond to one of the following situations by writing an essay stating your opinion.

1. One of your best friends has decided to drop out of high school. The friend claims that school is a waste of time. Think about the following questions:

    • Do you think this is a good idea? Why? Why not?

    • What will he/she gain by quitting?

    • What will he/she lose?

    Outline and write an essay in which you discuss these issues. In order to be convincing, you must support your point of view. Your own experience might be a good way to illustrate one of the paragraphs in the essay.

2. During a job interview, you are asked to write a description of your work experience. Do so by describing the jobs you have had in the past and what you have learned from each. For example, you might want to explain that babysitting taught you a sense of responsibility, the need for a thoughtful approach to a difficult situation, and a respect for the hard work it takes to do a good job. Or, working in a fast-food establishment may have helped you learn how to get along with difficult people, how to cooperate with others, and how to deal with pressure.

    You want this job. Be convincing.

3. How do you define the word *success*? What does it mean to you? Name a couple of successful people. What makes them successful? Is there more than one kind of success? What are they? What makes you feel successful? Brainstorm a list of words about success before you begin writing an essay about this subject. If you have trouble getting started, discuss success with a friend or family member.

4. You have been picked to participate in a yearlong project on another planet. Other than a change of clothes, you can take only one object. Would you take a picture of a friend or family member? Would you take a game of some sort? Would you take a book? Would you take a good-luck charm? Remember, you are going to be gone for one year. Write an essay in which you explain how you would make your decision, including what you would take and why.

Writing: A Comprehensive Guide to the Writing Process

Name _____ Date _____

Writing Narratives

Narratives tell stories and usually contain characters, a plot of some type, dialogue, and a setting. When you write a narrative, remember that the reader does not need to know every single detail. Some pointers are listed below, just to get you started.

1. Begin your story by describing the setting.

2. Continue by introducing your characters.

3. Begin the action. Set up the problem your characters face.

4. Have your characters interact through conversation and reactions to the situation.

5. Solve the problem.

Just sketching out answers to the above will get you started. Let's look at a sketch that Nina wrote.

1. The setting is a bus station late at night.

2. The characters are a sophisticated young woman and a worn-looking older woman.

3. Because of a bad storm, buses have been canceled. Both are uneasy about staying in the bus station all night, although reluctant to admit it.

4. As the bus station empties of passengers, the two very dissimilar women begin to talk.

5. They decide to take turns sleeping. When morning comes, they exchange addresses. Though dissimilar, they shared a problem that established a basis for a friendship.

Name _____   Date _____

 Exercise 9.4

Choose one of the following as a story starter.

1. Your best friend is a city person, used to the noise and confusion of a big city. She likes being busy, going to the movies, shopping, seeing new people. Suddenly, her family moves to a quiet country town where most people are farmers. What would happen? How would she react to the quiet? To the farm animals? To the lack of entertainment?

2. If your best friend is a country person, what would happen if that friend moved to a city? Proceed as in the previous situation.

3. Think about an event that changed your life or changed the way you look at the world. It may have been the death of someone close to you. It may have been the birth of a child. It may have been a much smaller event, like an overheard conversation or an unexpected call or gift. Tell your story. Since you are telling your own story, you may decide to talk directly to the reader, as in the following example:

   I had just closed the door to my apartment when I heard the ring of the telephone. In my hurry to answer it, I tripped over a stack of newspapers on the floor and fell face forward onto the arm of a chair. No big deal, you say. Think again. I ended up in the emergency room waiting for a doctor to stitch up the gash on my head. To make matters worse, I later learned that the phone call was about a job I wanted. Unable to reach me, my employer-to-be hired someone else.

4. Write the dialogue between two friends who have not seen each other in a couple of years. Each wants to impress the other with all that he/she has accomplished. Mention family, friends, job, interests.

Writing: A Comprehensive Guide to the Writing Process

Name _____   Date _____

Writing News Stories

News stories are about facts. The task of a reporter is that of a fact recorder. Pick up any newspaper and scan the paper for an interesting article. Read the article and underline responses to each of the following questions.

- Who is the article about?
- What happened?
- When did it happen?
- Where did it happen?
- Why did it happen?
- How did it happen?

How many paragraphs did you have to read to find this information? Read another story and follow the same procedure. Where did you find your answers? Probably in the first two or three paragraphs. Any background or further necessary information was supplied in later paragraphs. The reason for this is that busy people have little time. They want the basic information as quickly as possible. As a matter of fact, if you read the first three or four paragraphs of all of the front-page newspaper stories, you will be able to keep up to date.

Remember that the headline of a story should grab the reader's attention. You can do this by including action and descriptive words in your headline. Some examples are these:

charged	discovered
forced	fled
powerful	exploded
rushed	tremendous

Name _____   Date _____

 Exercise 9.5

Complete one of the following reporting assignments. Be sure to include the most important information in the first few paragraphs. Background information should be included after the Who? What? When? Where? Why? and How? questions are answered.

1. Write a news story about an upcoming event in your community, such as a political meeting, concert, or fund-raising event for a local charity. Search bulletin boards for notices of upcoming events. If further information is needed, call the organizers of the event. The entertainment section of the newspaper can also furnish information for this kind of story.

2. Interview a classmate who has recently moved to your hometown. After you have written about the five Ws/one H, describe your classmate's old home and present any interesting facts you have learned. (For help on developing questions, check out "Conducting and Recording Interviews" on page 97.)

3. Attend a meeting of a school, church, or civic organization. Write a report about the event.

4. Attend a sports event. Write a news story for the sports page of your local newspaper. Read a couple of sports stories before you begin writing.

5. Watch a favorite television show. Take notes on the action and characters complete enough to jog your memory when you sit down to write. Remember, as a reporter your job is to present accurate information. Write a news story based on this material.

6. Write an obituary for a famous historical character. An encyclopedia, a history book, or the Internet will supply needed facts.

Name _____ Date _____

Journal Writing

Journal

 A journal is a written record of events, thoughts, or ideas, often written in the first person—with "I" as the recorder.

Most of us are so busy that we have little time to think about the passing of each day. By writing in a journal, you can keep a record of each day and have something to look back on. Writers keep journals for many reasons. Some writers keep idea journals in which they write story ideas, descriptions of characters, interesting news notes, as well as conversations they overhear. Some people keep dream journals, where they describe vivid dreams or disturbing nightmares. In fact, many well-known authors keep journals and a pen on their bedside tables so they may note particularly interesting dream facts. Many people write daily entries in their journals (or diaries) recording the events of their lives. Probably you have read portions of *The Diary of a Young Girl* by Anne Frank. Although Anne called her book a diary, it went beyond being only a record of daily life. What makes her writing so interesting is that she thought about and reacted to everything around her.

Here are some practical ideas about journal keeping. It isn't necessary to have a fancy hardcover book in which to write your journal entries. Your words can be just as effective saved on a computer disk or written in a spiral-bound notebook. Select the type of book that works best for you. Plan to date each entry, and write on a fairly regular basis. You need not write every day, but try for once a week. Don't limit your journal to writing; feel free to illustrate. Be creative: You are, after all, writing a book.

Name _____ Date _____

 Exercise 9.6

Use one of the following ideas to spur the creation of a journal of your own.

1. Keep a movie or television journal by writing down your reactions to particular shows in your journal book. Be sure to include titles and names of characters. People often watch a movie or television program and remember nothing about what they have seen. Doesn't that seem like a waste of time?

2. Keep an observation journal. You might observe and record the actions of animals in your environment. You might record the changes you see in the seasons.

3. Keep a daily journal of work you have completed.

4. Keep a journal with comments on the books you are reading.

5. Keep a daily journal of the activities of family members.

6. Begin a house journal in which you describe any completed repairs or improvements.

7. Keep a journal of favorite family stories. Include stories about the cooks in your family.

8. Keep an "I don't understand" journal containing ideas that confuse you. By writing them down, you will find it easier to explain your problems to someone else.

9. Keep a travel journal. Record where you have been, when, why, and what happened.

10. Keep a dream or nightmare journal. Place your journal by your bed so that you can write before you forget your dream.

Most Important—Keep a journal, a permanent record of your journey through life.

Writing: A Comprehensive Guide to the Writing Process

Name _____   Date _____

Writing Advertisements

Advertisement

 An advertisement is an appeal to a target audience to look favorably upon (and usually to purchase) a given product or service.

What is your favorite ad? Why does it grab your attention? Since you are going to be writing advertisements, you need to think about these questions. Advertising is expensive, and ad writers can't afford to waste words. You must decide on the best possible audience for your product, and then you must appeal to that audience in the most effective way. Consider how television advertisements work. Would you agree that many depend on color, action, and a recognizable spokesperson? Since you will probably not have the wonders of television at your fingertips, to sell your product you need to consider words that can have a powerful impact on your audience. One of the most effective words in the language is **sale**. People have a hard time turning away from a sale. Other words that draw attention are *bargain, free, bonus, once-in-a-lifetime opportunity*. These are all powerful words.

Another point to consider when writing an advertisement is what makes people want a particular item. Many people enjoy being "in the know," that is, following the latest trends. These are the people who always see the latest movies, try every new food product, wear the latest styles, and follow the leadership of trendsetters.

Brand names also play a part in advertising. People from all over the world recognize the names Pepsi and Coke. Advertising has paid off in a big way for these companies, as their brand names have become household words. There was a time when brand names appeared only on labels. Today, you will see brand names on everything—from shoes to hats. That benefits advertisers in two ways: Customers buy their products, and customers advertise their products. What a deal!

Name _____ Date _____

 Exercise 9.7

There is much to consider when you write an ad. To review quickly:

1. Use powerful words appealing to the audience you have selected.

2. Capitalize on the product's fad appeal.

3. Mention brand names.

Now, write an ad for one of these scenarios:

1. Write an advertisement offering your writing skills to students who are having trouble in writing class. Emphasize your strengths and your interest in helping others.

2. Write an advertisement to sell your collection of *National Geographic* magazines. Emphasize the quality of the educational material available in these magazines. Feel free to mention particularly interesting articles. Appeal to parents anxious to help their kids.

3. You have just developed a wonderful sandwich. You are convinced that it is exactly what the American public wants and needs. Before you write your ad, determine what audience will be most interested in your particular sandwich. Are you going to appeal to vegetarians? Meat eaters? Dieters? You decide.

4. You have been left a fantastic fortune by an unknown benefactor. At last you will be able to open the restaurant of your dreams. Write a paragraph about your restaurant and then write an advertisement announcing its opening. Be sure to consider your audience.

5. Your family has decided to have a tag sale. Unfortunately, you have learned that five other families in your neighborhood have picked the same day for their sales. Write an ad that will draw people to your sale first.

6. You need a job badly. Write an ad highlighting your special talents.

Writing: A Comprehensive Guide to the Writing Process

Name _____ Date _____

Conducting and Recording Interviews

Interview

 An interview is a conversation, usually in question-and-answer format, in which one or more people request information from another source.

You may wonder what interviewing has to do with writing. Interviews can play two very important roles in the world of writing. First, interviewing a person with knowledge of a particular subject or event can be the basis for an interesting piece of writing. Second, using quotations from a knowledgeable person can add credibility to your writing. For example, an interview with a veteran of World War II or with a person who remembers the war would make any paper you write about it more real. A first-person experience report of any event adds human interest and excitement to a story. Beginning an essay or article with such a quotation also draws readers' attention.

Whenever you conduct an interview, approach the interview as a professional reporter might do.

1. Explain the reasons for the interview to the person you wish to question.

2. Set up a time and meeting place.

3. If you want to tape-record the interview, ask for permission.

4. Prior to the interview, write out your questions. You don't want to forget important details.

5. Be on time for the interview. Begin the interview by discussing the project you are working on.

6. Move on to your questions.

7. At the end of the interview, thank the person for his/her time and information. Afterwards, write a thank you letter.

Probably the most important characteristic of a good reporter is the ability to listen. After you have asked a question, give your interviewee plenty of time to respond. Most important, listen. Listen carefully. Try to link what has been said to your next question. If your interviewee is having trouble, encourage the person to speak. Lead-ins and such questions as the following help: "As you said before," "What happened then?" "Were you surprised when this happened?" If you are not taping, take careful notes. It is up to you to quote the person accurately. You owe it to that person and to your readers to present reliable information.

When the time comes to write, be sure to include sufficient background information to convince your readers that you are quoting a trustworthy source. After identifying the person, give a brief description of his/her background and your reasons for interviewing this person. You will probably paraphrase (restate in your own words) much of the information you use, but include quotations that are particularly interesting, unusual, or well stated. Remember that direct quotations must be enclosed in quotation marks.

      Writing: A Comprehensive Guide to the Writing Process

Name _____ Date _____

 Exercise 9.8

You may want to improve your interviewing skills by conducting a practice interview with someone in your classroom or your family before trying your hand in other interview situations.

1. Write a paper on a typical day in the life of someone in your class or your family. Request an interview. Set a time. Develop some questions. Conduct the interview. You may write up the interview as dialogue between you and the person, or you may use the interview as the basis for an essay, using an occasional quotation to lend credibility to your work.

2. You have been asked to write about the changes in your community or neighborhood in the past five, ten, or fifteen years. Interview a classmate or a member of your family. You may have to prompt the person you are interviewing by asking some of the following questions:

   • Are there any new buildings in the area?

   • What changes have you seen in the area?

   • Have any of your close friends moved away?

   • Do you remember any special events that took place here?

   • How would you change the area if you could?

3. Interview someone engaged in a profession that interests you. Find out what this person's advice is to a student who wishes to enter the profession.

4. Interview a collector of some kind. It might be someone who collects baseball cards, old tools, sheet music, cars, or books. Ask the following questions:

   • What started you collecting?

   • How large is your collection?

   • What is needed to make the collection complete?

   • What is your most prized piece?

   • Where can I go to find out more about this type of collecting?

(continued)

Writing: A Comprehensive Guide to the Writing Process

Name _____   Date _____

5. Interview a person responsible for doing some type of training. You might interview someone who teaches a drivers' education course, who trains animals, or who trains new employees for a local business. Ask the trainer to describe his/her most interesting and most frustrating experiences with trainees.

6. Interview someone who has traveled to another city, state, country. Ask the person to describe the location and answer the following questions:

   • Why did you visit this place? Had friends told you about it?

   • What kinds of entertainment are offered there?

   • Is the weather like that of your hometown?

   • What are the local landmarks?

   • Do any famous people live in the area?

   Present the information as you would in an article for the travel section of your newspaper.

Name _____ Date _____

Preparing an Oral Report

Sooner or later you are going to have to speak to a group of people. Yes, you! You may have to give a report in class. A friend may ask you to propose a toast at a wedding reception. You may want to act as a spokesperson for a group of friends or neighbors. There are dozens of occasions when you will have to get on your feet and speak. Not to worry. The planning and organizational skills you have learned as part of your writing assignments are exactly what you need to plan an oral presentation. Being able to stand up and talk with people is a powerful tool, one you want to have in your toolbox of skills. Approach the preparation of any oral presentation as you would the development of an essay.

1. Consider your audience members. What are their interests?

2. Consider your purpose. Are you trying to entertain, to persuade, or to inform?

3. Write down words that come to mind as you brainstorm your purpose.

4. Write a good, clean rough draft.

5. Revise, proofread, and rewrite. This time, triple-space your material, and key or write it in large letters to make it easy to read.

6. Read your material aloud at least once a day for several days.

A couple of days before your presentation, read your material aloud to a friend or family member. If you have followed these steps, you will know your material well enough so that you won't have to read every word from the paper. Your goal will be to establish occasional eye contact with your listeners. By establishing eye contact with your audience, you are saying, "I'm not talking at you; I am speaking with you."

If you have a chance, watch a news program covering a speech by some well-known person. I'm not talking about someone like the president, who usually has a television prompter; I'm talking about someone who obviously has a written statement on the lectern. Notice how the speaker looks down, reads a few words, and then looks up to complete a sentence. This will take practice, but the practice pays off.

As any public speaker will tell you, take every opportunity offered to speak in front of a group. Each time you speak, you will feel a bit more at ease. Practice makes successful athletes. It works for speakers too. Honest!

Writing: A Comprehensive Guide to the Writing Process

Name _____   Date _____

 Exercise 9.9

Use one of the following as the topic for an oral report.

1. If you like to eat, you probably like to talk about food. Since you are not alone, food is a great subject for an oral report. How about describing a typical family meal at your house? Do you all sit down together, or does everyone eat different things at different times? Another approach to this subject is to describe a holiday meal or your cooking specialty. Bringing in samples is a surefire way of pleasing your audience.

2. Some people have pets. Some people have pet plants. Present an oral report on the advantages of having pet plants. Among other things, point out that they don't eat much, they don't require exercise, and they are not messy. Don't forget to mention what they do need—water, for one.

3. If you dread speaking to an audience, there is a perfect subject for you: Talk about what you had to go through to prepare for this oral report. Mention your fear of the words *oral report*. Describe the jitters you feel. Talk about what happened the last time you spoke to a group. To get your audience involved, pass out a survey. Tell them no names are needed. Here are some possible questions.

   • Do you enjoy public speaking?

   • Why? Why not?

   • How do you prepare to speak to a group?

   • What is the best advice you can give to a speaker?

   Everyone likes to be asked for advice. If you have time, discuss some of the answers.

Writing: A Comprehensive Guide to the Writing Process

Name _____   Date _____

Writing Letters

Many people feel that in this day of e-mail, fax machines, and voice mail, there is little need for letter writing. However, you may still want to write at least two kinds of letters: friendly letters and business letters. Although technology has made communication easier, it will never replace letter writing for a variety of reasons. First, a letter is more personal than an electronic note—it takes a little more time, thought, and just plain physical involvement than does machine-produced print. Second, it comes directly from the writer's hands. Third, it is part of a distinguished tradition reaching back through the centuries. If you have ever found an old handwritten letter, you know what I mean. Imagine, it is possible to go to a museum and look at a piece of paper that George Washington held in his hands in the eighteenth century.

Friendly Letters

Of the two main types of letters, friendly letters are more informal. Friendly letters include a heading consisting of your address and the date (many write just the date), a greeting, the letter itself, and a closing. The friendly letter can include family news and activities, questions and comments, and informal language. One specific type of friendly letter is what used to be called a "bread and butter" letter. This type of letter was written to thank a host and hostess for meals. People also sent "bread and butter" letters after a party, a weekend visit, or after receiving gifts and other favors. Personal letters are also sent to congratulate a friend on a promotion or a new baby. Finally, personal notes are sent in response to the death of an acquaintance. Obviously, you can always buy a commercially printed card, but isn't it better to show how much you care by taking the time to write your own message?

When you sit down to write a friendly letter, plan on writing a rough draft as you would for a writing assignment. This will give you an opportunity to get the words down without worrying about punctuation, grammar, and mechanics. How to begin? Brainstorm. What is it you want to say? Why? Get your ideas down on paper first. Then, worry about smoothing out your work. Be sure to include specifics. If you are thanking someone for a delicious meal, mention what you particularly enjoyed. If you are thanking someone for a visit, discuss memorable activities. If you are congratulating someone, do it!

If someone dies, writing a sympathy letter to the family is appropriate. This is probably the most difficult kind of personal letter to write, but the family needs to know that others care. Tell them exactly how you feel. You can include an "I'll never forget when . . ." statement if you choose. Fill in the sentence with something you remember about the person. What you are saying by doing this is that this person will be missed but not forgotten.

Whenever you put off writing a letter, whatever kind of friendly letter it may be, think about how much you like receiving them.

Writing: A Comprehensive Guide to the Writing Process

Name _____   Date _____

Business Letters

Letters in which any type of business is discussed are more formal and should be written in a proper business form. This includes the following:

1. A full heading—your complete address, followed by the date

2. The inside address—the name and address of the person to whom you are writing

3. A salutation—the hello of the letter

4. The body of the letter

5. A closing and a typed signature line below a space for your written signature

If additional material is accompanying the letter—like a check, money order, or resume—note this two lines below your typed signature line by writing "Enc." or "Enclosure". If you are enclosing more than one document, write "Enclosures".

 Exercise 9.10

Analyzing a Business Letter

Study and label the parts of the business letter on the next page. Note the heading including the writer's address and the date. It is followed by four lines of space and then the inside address—the name and address of the person who will receive the letter. One more line is left blank before the salutation. The salutation of a business letter is followed by a colon, whereas a comma follows the salutation of a friendly letter.

One line of space is left before the first word of the body of the letter is written. You will also notice the double space between the body of the letter and the closing. It is correct to leave three blank lines between the closing and the typed signature line. The space between the closing and signature line allows room for the writer's handwritten signature. Notice that every line of this letter begins at the left margin. Although there are other correct letter formats, this "block form" seems to be the one most frequently used.

Now that you have reviewed the layout of the letter, what about the content? Notice how the writer informs Mrs. Umbro that she knows of the Umbro Company and also notes how she learned of the job opening. This approach is a good one to use when writing a letter like this. Also, notice how she ties in her experience with the requirements of the job. When writing this type of letter, always match your credentials to the needs of employers. If you examine the letter carefully, you will note that the language is formal and polite. Remember, when you write a business letter, you want to be as professional as possible.

    Writing: A Comprehensive Guide to the Writing Process

Name _____ Date _____

Now read the letter and label the heading, inside address, salutation, body of the letter, closing, and signature line.

---

565 Wallace Street
Potsdam, NY 13678
April 17, 2000

Mrs. Vita Umbro, Manager
The Umbro Company
P.O. Box 678
Austin, TX 78767

Dear Mrs. Umbro:

For several years, I have been reading about the effort the Umbro Company has put into improving the lives of the elderly in the Austin area. When Mr. Rudolph Lu of Employment Possibilities told me that you had a position open for an activities director, I was immediately interested.

I began volunteering at a local residential facility for senior citizens when I was in middle school. It was then that I learned how much older people have to offer to those who take the time to listen. My volunteer work included helping with meals, reading to those who could not see well, and organizing and playing games with groups of residents. After receiving my GED two years ago, I began work as an aide at a local residential center where, in addition to my other work, I helped the activity director plan and organize activities for the residents. I think I am now ready to use my experience to benefit another group of people.

I would appreciate an opportunity to meet with you as soon as possible. I may be reached at the above address or at 512-268-4135. Thank you.

Sincerely,

Kristina Lichtenberger

Name _____   Date _____

 Exercise 9.11

Write a letter based on one of the following scenarios.

1. Read through the employment advertisements in your local newspaper. Select an ad of interest to you. Write a letter applying for the job. Use the format presented on pages 103 and 104.

2. You have just spent a weekend at the home of an out-of-state friend. Write a letter to the friend and to the friend's parents, thanking them for the good time you had. This is an informal letter.

3. You recently purchased a defective product from a local store. Write to the home office of this store explaining why you should receive a replacement. The local store refused to replace the product because it was bought on sale. Make up a product and a store name. Remember, it is always good to begin any letter on a positive note. In this case, you might mention how happy you have been with past purchases. Use the business letter format.

4. You have been asked to write a letter of recommendation for a fellow employee. Write a letter in which you describe this person as cooperative and hard working. Try to give an example of both of these characteristics in a formal letter.

5. An old family friend is in the hospital in a distant city. Write an informal letter filled with comments on your family and friends. Include information on what you have been doing.

6. Your English teacher has asked you to write him or her an informal letter explaining what grade you should receive for the course. Name that grade and offer specific evidence supporting it.

      Writing: A Comprehensive Guide to the Writing Process

Name _____   Date _____

Writing Book Reports

Do you like mysteries? Science fiction? Horror? Are romantic relationships on the fogbound coast of Maine of interest? Do you like interplanetary exploration, or do you want panoramic descriptions and stories based on fascinating moments in history? Events that interest you are the events you should highlight when writing a book report. Don't be content with sketching out the plot and naming the characters. Make the book live by focusing on what made it a good read for you. On the other hand, you are not going to like every book you read. If you found a book uninspiring, be honest about it.

The next time you are asked to do a book report, try the following steps:

If You Liked the Book

1. Describe the setting of the book.

2. Write a brief synopsis of the plot.

3. Describe the problem(s) that the characters face.

4. Quote a particularly well-written passage. Include the page number.

5. Conclude by explaining why you are recommending the book. Try to compare it with another book or movie you have liked.

If You Didn't Like the Book

1. Begin by explaining why you didn't like it.

2. Write a brief synopsis of the plot.

3. Give specific information about the setting.

4. Describe why the characters or plot were unsatisfactory.

5. Quote a poorly written passage.

6. Mention how the book could be improved.

Writing: A Comprehensive Guide to the Writing Process

Name _____ Date _____

 Exercise 9.12

If you want to try a different type of book report, use one of the ideas below.

1. Write a letter from one of the characters in the novel to the author. The character's position is that he/she has been treated unfairly by the author. Describe situations in the book proving that the character didn't get enough attention. Then explain how the author should have handled the character.

2. Select a character from the book you are discussing. Write a series of journal entries that character might have written. Think about how the character might have felt in some of the situations described in the book.

3. Develop a series of letters between two minor characters in the book. The letters can explain how they view the actions of the major characters.

4. You have been asked to interview one of the characters in the book. Develop a list of questions you would like to ask. Then, supply the answers you think the character might provide.

Sample Questions

- Do you think you were treated fairly by the other characters in the book?
- If you could change one thing about your appearance as described in the book, what would you change?
- Which of the other characters do you like or dislike? Why?

---

5. Write a letter to the author about some part of the book that puzzles you. Use a business letter format. If possible, mail the letter in care of the book's publisher.

Writing: A Comprehensive Guide to the Writing Process

Name _____   Date _____

Answering Essay Questions

Do you quake at the idea of taking an essay test? Would you rather stay home on test day, going only because you know you will have to face this punishment sooner or later? Rather than worry, do something about test taking. Plan a study strategy that has you entering the classroom with some degree of confidence.

- Go over your notes, underlining areas the teacher emphasized. Compare your notes with those of a friend.

- Review all the quizzes you have taken in this class.

- With a friend's help, write out questions you think might be asked. Then, take your own test.

When test time arrives, you are ready. Read the directions! Read them again! Many students do poorly because they do not pay attention to the directions for taking the test. Always read and reread, underlining important words like these:

- Give an example

- Define

- Give facts

- Compare and contrast

- List

Then, do what is asked. Notice that each of these terms refers to a way writers develop paragraphs. All you are doing in your answer is writing what you believe is correct and supporting it with examples, definitions, or facts.

Take time to plan your answer to each question. *Brainstorm* words you connect with the key words in the question. Jot down a brief *outline* of your answer, just as you would if you were writing an essay for class. Although time-consuming, this preparation will pay off in an organized response to the question.

Writing test essays poses the same challenge as writing essays for class. You must consider your audience and purpose and then organize and write an answer containing the requested information.

Writing: A Comprehensive Guide to the Writing Process

Name _____   Date _____

 Exercise 9.13

Practice your test-taking skills by answering the questions below. Read the directions carefully, and underline key words. Don't forget to brainstorm and plan the organization of your answer. Remember:

- Give an example—state a specific fact or event
- Define—state the meaning of a term
- Give facts—state specific information
- Compare and contrast—tell how things are both alike and different
- Describe—show
- Explain—give reasons

1. How do you feel about test taking? Read the passage below and compare and contrast your test-taking reactions.

    > Even before I got out of bed, I felt a little sick. I had a feeling of dread that I couldn't explain. I drank a little juice but couldn't manage to choke down even a piece of toast. As the hands of the clock moved towards 8:00 A.M., I knew I had to leave for school and the test. The test! I had been dreading it for weeks. I just had to do well; so much depended on it.

2. Sara Teasdale wrote poetry during the early part of the twentieth century. Four lines of her poem "The Coin" are quoted below. Read the lines carefully once or twice. Think about what "heart's treasury" means. What do these lines mean to you? Explain, and give an example from your own experience.

 Into my heart's treasury
I slipped a coin
That time cannot take
Or thief purloin.

3. Describe your approach to preparing for a test. Be specific.

4. What advice would you give a new student? Explain what the student needs to know about this school and the students in it. Give examples. Describe the advantages and disadvantages of going to school here.

A Final Word:
Evaluating Written Work

One of the hardest tasks a teacher faces is grading written work that students have labored over. As we all know, a low grade can discourage hesitant writers and make it impossible for them to forge ahead. Using the student informational pages in this book will help students gain the confidence they need by providing clear-cut expectations. You, the teacher, can also use their checklists as a basis for your grading. You can use the traditional *A* to mark work that meets all requirements and lesser grades for lesser accomplishment.

If you have collected your students' work in writing folders, you may want to insert a grading sheet in each folder. On this sheet, list the assignments that require completion during each marking period. Next to each assignment, mark the grade received and any comments that might help the student.

The emphasis today in grading is on performance-based assessment. Even though you may hesitate to use this type of grading, this is a good time to begin thinking about moving in that direction. To help you, I have collected a series of grading statements you may find useful. Pick and choose the ones which fit into your work.

- The student's writing is clear, concise, and imaginative.
- The student has developed each topic sentence.

- The student has followed all directions.
- The student has used a variety of correct sentences.
- The student has made no more than ____ mechanical errors.
- The student has a strong introduction.
- The student has clearly stated the purpose of the paper.
- The student has developed paragraphs in a variety of ways.
- The student has organized the material in a logical way.
- The student has used correct capitalization.
- The student has no more than ____ spelling errors.
- The student has used appropriate language.
- The student has exhibited a knowledge of the subject.

As you can see, each of these statements describes the ideal. It would be a simple matter to work from these statements to statements describing less competent work. An example follows:

- The student's writing is clear, concise, and imaginative.
- The student's writing is understandable, but wordy and unimaginative.
- The student's writing is confusing.

(continued)

110

A Final Word:
Evaluating Written Work *(continued)*

You can use a similar approach in evaluating portfolios, collections of student work, and other supportive materials, like maps, charts, surveys, and illustrations.

An interesting approach to evaluation is to have both the student and the teacher use the same tool. You will find an example of such a tool on page 112.

All the teacher has to do is change the subject of each sentence to include the student's name. If this technique is to be effective, teachers must meet with students to discuss the responses of each.

We teachers have come a long way in our approach to grading. I can remember receiving my first corrected college essay. It was a sea of red without suggestions for improvement or words of encouragement. Fortunately, we now see that if our students are to become writers, we, as teachers, can do at least two things to help them.

1. Clarify our expectations. Students need to know what is expected of them.

2. Encourage. There is something good in every piece of written work.

A Final Word:
Evaluating Written Work

Evaluation Tool

At the end of each quarter, you will be asked to evaluate the work in your portfolio based on the following statements. I will use the same sheet to evaluate your work. Later we can compare our answers.

Assign +4 for excellent work.

+3 indicates the item needs a little more attention.

+2 indicates the work is barely adequate.

+1 means that some of the assignments need immediate improvement.

−1 means you need to rewrite and reorganize.

---

1. I have completed every assignment.

2. My assignments are organized by dates with the most recent date on top.

3. I've written a variety: letters, essays, book reports, etc.

4. My rough drafts show I have revised and proofread.

5. I have included some extra pieces that were not assigned.

6. My portfolio contains a list of future projects.

Answer Key

Part I: The Writing Process

Exercise 1.1 (p. 6)

Accept a wide range of answers.

Exercise 1.2 (p. 7)

Accept a wide range of answers. The purpose of this activity is simply to get students writing.

Exercise 2.1 (p. 9)

In this exercise, students have been asked to match nouns with appropriate verbs, adjectives, and adverbs. Accept any appropriate answers. This exercise can be fun as well as instructive if you allow a little more latitude than with other activities.

Exercise 2.2 (p. 11)

Accept a wide range of answers.

Exercise 2.3 (p. 11)

Many answers are possible; here are some suggestions.

1. The ship sank in the harbor during a severe storm.
2. Traffic was heavy in the morning.
3. We ate dinner at 6:30 P.M.
4. Trees fell across the street.
5. The computer crashed to the floor.
6. He removed the disk from the desk.
7. The river flooded during a week of rain.
8. The audience cheered during the concert.
9. The fire burned for several hours.
10. Musicians played at the dance.

Exercise 2.4 (p. 13)

As long as the pronouns refer back to a reasonable subject, accept all answers.

Exercise 2.5 (p. 14)

Many answers are possible; here are some suggestions.

1. Juan held a black book in his hands while talking with a friend.
2. Erin was pleased because the concert was not canceled.
3. As Karl walked by the open door, he saw a man watching him.
4. Lyle was alone in the deserted house, listening to the howling wind.
5. As I walked around the lake, I saw a large bird sitting on a rock.

Exercise 2.6 (p. 17)

Accept a wide range of answers. If students have trouble, use the following paragraph as an example:

Although we take bags for granted, where would we be without them? Think of the student who has to carry everything from books to bologna sandwiches, the businessperson who has a stack of papers to keep organized, or even the traveler who is going away for a week. Each of them would be lost without a bag. Bags may be simple objects, but they are necessary.

Exercise 2.7 (p. 17)

Students will choose a variety of shows. Accept a wide range of answers. Look for such reasons as these:

informative, entertaining, lively, up-to-date, strong characters, action, good guests, setting, funny, the people, the plot, different, the technology, exciting.

Exercise 2.8 (p. 19)

Accept a wide variety of answers.

Exercise 3.1 (p. 22)

1. swiftly, silently
2. day, dawned, dread
3. tramped, through, toward; fens, farmland
4. delayed, deterred
5. rioters, ripped; city, center

Exercise 3.2 (p. 23)

Many answers are possible; here are some suggestions.

1. The tall trees swayed quietly back and forth in the forest.
2. There were twelve types of ice cream listed.
3. Mr. Lu rushed home through thick traffic.
4. The frightened bank clerk deliberately dropped to his knees as the alarm sounded.

Exercise 3.3 (p. 24)

Many answers are possible; here are some suggestions.

1. The rusty gate creaked.
2. The pizza was sizzling.
3. They jumped into the rushing river.
4. The machinery groaned loudly.
5. We heard the sound of tooting horns and screeching brakes.

6. Thick cobwebs covered the dark entrance to the cave.
7. Ricardo cautiously walked toward the deserted house.

Exercise 3.4 (p. 25)

1. <u>That was a good time;</u> hard work is seldom considered a good time.
2. <u>Oh, wonderful;</u> lightning and thunder are dangerous, not wonderful.
3. <u>The lionhearted hunter;</u> a hunter with the heart of a lion would not be scared by a mouse.
4. <u>He had never touched first base;</u> by missing first base he missed a home run.
5. <u>It's nothing . . . 56-page report;</u> a 56-page report is a substantial offering, not "nothing."

Exercise 3.5 (p. 26)

Many answers are possible; here are some suggestions.

1. spring water—clear, fresh, pure, cold
2. snow—cold, white, fresh, soft
3. knife—sharp, hard, shiny
4. asphalt—black, rough, hard, strong-smelling
5. granite—grey, hard, enduring, glacial

Exercise 3.6 (p. 27)

Many answers are possible; here are some suggestions.

1. wet—air in August, a boat deck in a squall
2. cold—a dog's nose, a steel post in winter
3. hard—water in Antarctica, a stalactite
4. thick—dandelions in a lawn, tourists on a summer Saturday
5. gentle—dust falling, time passing, a moth's antennae

Exercise 3.7 (p. 27)

Many answers are possible; here are some suggestions.

1. The child was as thoughtful as a mother would be.
2. Summer is like a slowly developing dream.
3. The moon is like a silver apple.
4. The weather is as changeable as some people's minds.
5. Friendship is like a warm blanket.
6. Good friends are like a safe place.
7. Her remarks are as sharp as an axe.
8. He ran as fast as a deer.
9. The book is as dull as dirt.

Exercise 4.1 (p. 35)

Accept a wide range of answers.

Exercise 4.2 (p. 37)

Accept a wide range of answers.

Exercise 4.3 (p. 39)

Answers will vary widely.

Exercise 4.4 (p. 40)

before, however, below

Exercise 4.5 (p. 41)

Paragraph 1—first, next, add, now, after
Paragraph 2—as, across, in front, on, to my right, in the background, left, in front
Paragraph 3—thus, as a result

Exercise 5.1 (p. 45)

Following are the problems that should be addressed in any revision:

The paragraph is unfocused. The student mentions interests only in passing. Sentence 2 has too many "ands." Rewrite as three sentences. Most of the sentences are awkward. The writer doesn't say anything. The writer has answered the "who" and "what," but there is no "when," "where," "why," or "how." The writer is saying he/she isn't happy with the teacher. I would like to know what "stuff" is.

Exercise 5.2 (p. 50)

Answers are in the text.

Exercise 5.3 (p. 51)

Paragraph will vary. Check to be sure both similarities and differences are noted. With all this information, students should have no problems.

Exercise 5.4 (p. 51)

1. The subject of the paragraph is Saturdays.
2. The writer seems to prefer "free" Saturdays.
3. The writer says what he or she does on each type of Saturday.
4. No. The writer could have mentioned that he or she doesn't have to go to school on any type of Saturday.
5. The writer developed the paragraph with examples.

Exercise 5.5 (p. 52)

If students have trouble deciding what to write about, suggest they brainstorm one of the following: a special Saturday, Saturday at my house, company Saturdays, Saturday jobs, wasted Saturdays.

Exercise 5.6 (p. 54)

Accept appropriate examples from a current newspaper.

Exercise 5.7 (p. 56)

Some suggestions follow:

1. Found Food Foils Hunger
2. Chef Cooks Cabbage Competently
3. Hitty Hits Again
4. A Fence Couldn't Keep Him In

Exercise 6.1 (p. 61)

Beautiful People

1. Change *due* to *do*
2. Change *mine* to *mind*
3. Change *express* to *expression, know* to *known*
4. Change *wood* to *would, then* to *than*
5. No errors
6. Change *pour* to *poor*
7. No errors
8. No errors

With one exception, all errors in this paragraph were homophone errors. Students who missed these would benefit by adding these confusing words to their checklists.

Exercise 6.2 (p. 62)

Remembering Miss Otis

1. Change *street* to *Street, say* to *saw*
2. No error
3. Commas needed after petunia and pansy (Some writers leave out the comma after pansy. If you decide to do so, be consistent.)
4. No error
5. No error
6. Comma after bracelet (See 3 above.)
7. No error
8. Change *eye lashes* to *eyelashes*

9. addition, (The comma is used for clarification.)
10. Change *though* to *thought*
11. makeup?
12. Change *answer* to *answers* (Questions is plural.)
13. No error

The emphasis in this passage is on punctuation. Students should make needed additions to their checklists.

Exercise 6.3 (p. 64)

Blue and Other Colorful Words

1. No error
2. it, (Dependent clause at the beginning of a sentence requires a comma.)
3. No error
4. repetition becomes reputation followed by a ? situations?
5. No error
6. No error
7. furious, (See 2 above.)
8. "red-handed," and (Compound sentence joined by a conjunction requires a comma.)

In this activity, punctuation is stressed. You might want to review dependent clauses if students fail to recognize the clauses in this section.

Part II: Audience and Purpose

Exercise 8.1 (p. 72)

Answers will vary.

Exercise 8.2 (p. 74)

Many answers are possible.

Exercise 8.3 (p. 75)

Many answers are possible.

Exercise 8.4 (p. 76)

Many answers are possible.

Exercise 8.5 (p. 77)

Answers will vary, but should resemble the following:

1. The mouse ran past the cat, which was lying by the fire.
2. World War I started in 1914.
3. Our football team lost about half the games it played this season.
4. To load paper into the copier, pull out the paper drawer.
5. Colombia is a country in South America.

Exercise 8.6 (p. 78)

Introduce this activity by bringing in a current magazine and discussing each of the questions as they apply to it. When you arrive at #7, mention other magazines that are designed for special groups. For example, *Time* is for people interested in general news; *Psychology Today* is for people who analyze behavior; *Prevention* is designed for people who want to remain healthy.

Exercise 8.7 (p. 80)

1. Yes. He mentions the date of Patriots' Day, the Revolutionary War connection, and a specific poem by Henry Wadsworth Longfellow.
2. He tries to be persuasive by mentioning that poetry helps students to think and remember.
3. Narrative writing is story telling. The letter tells the beginning of the Paul Revere story.
4. Although the writer uses narrative, informative, and persuasive detail, I believe the writer is trying to be persuasive. He is trying to convince people that students should memorize poetry. Support: past generations remember history; poetry makes history memorable; educational practices of the past worked.
5. He is trying to reach a broad audience, but parents and older people are those who might accept his arguments.

Part III: Exploring the Writing World

Exercise 9.1 (p. 85)

Answers will vary. An example is presented in the text.

Exercise 9.2 (p. 87)

I. Active people
   A. Swimming
   B. Running
   C. Biking
   D. Stretching
   E. Walking
II. Couch potatoes
   A. Watching television
   B. Reading magazines
   C. Watching movies
   D. Listening to the radio
   E. Sitting

Exercise 9.3 (p. 88)

Essay Ideas—Suggestions for ways in which to develop essays 3 and 4 are listed below.

3. Students may think of success as money and fame. Ask them to consider people in their daily lives who are successful in other ways too.
4. Ask students to brainstorm a list of their most prized possessions. Then ask them to write sentences about each. The last step toward discovering their topic is to look at which of the sentences they found the easiest

to write. This is where their writing should begin.

Exercise 9.4 (p. 90)

Students' narratives should contain a plot of some kind in chronological order. Also, dialogue should be included. Overkill tends to be the problem in narratives; writers want to include too much unnecessary detail. If students have this problem, show them examples of concise narratives. Hemingway works well, especially his short stories.

Exercise 9.5 (p. 92)

As long as students stick to the five Ws and an H, they will not have trouble with this assignment.

Exercise 9.6 (p. 94)

Journals should be an ongoing assignment. Begin the school year by asking students to select the type of journal they wish to keep. Allow class time twice a week for journal writing. Plan to read and respond to the journals at least once a quarter. Use E for excellent (complete), G for good (one assignment missing), S for satisfactory (two assignments missing), and N for needs more work.

Exercise 9.7 (p. 96)

Answers will vary, but all three items on the checklist should be covered.

Exercise 9.8 (p. 98)

Remind your students that every item mentioned in each of these assignments must be covered in their finished interview. Evaluate accordingly. Before students actually conduct interviews, take class time for them to role-play their interviews with another student. Discuss their questions to weed out any that might prove embarrassing for the interviewee. If you assign question 6, you might want to make a copy of a travel article for students to discuss before developing their own.

Exercise 9.9 (p. 101)

Oral reports frighten the most confident among us. Something about standing up in front of our peers turns many of us into quivering wrecks. Help your students by having them practice in front of small groups before appearing before the entire class.

Exercise 9.10 (p. 103)

heading —	565 Wallace Street Potsdam, NY 13678 April 17, 2000
inside address —	Mrs. Vita Umbro, Manager The Umbro Company P.O. Box 678 Austin, TX 78767
salutation —	Dear Mrs. Umbro:
body of the letter —	For several years, I have been reading about the effort the Umbro Company has put into improving the lives of the elderly in the Austin area. When Mr. Rudolph Lu of Employment Possibilities told me that you had a position open for an activities director, I was immediately interested. I began volunteering at a local residential facility for senior citizens when I was in middle school. It was then that I learrned how much older people have to offer to those who take the time to listen. My volunteer work included helping with meals, reading to those who could not see well, and organizing and playing games with groups of residents. After receiving my GED two years ago, I began work as an aide at a local residential center where, in addition to my other work, I helped the activity director plan and organize activities for the residents. I think I am now ready to use my experience to benefit another group of people. I would appreciate an opportunity to meet with you as soon as possible. I may be reached at the above address or at 512-268-4135. Thank you.
closing —	Sincerely, — space for signature
typed signature line —	Kristina Lichtenberger

Exercise 9.11 (p. 105)

The assignments on this page are a blend of formal and informal letter-writing situations. Numbers 1, 3, 4, 6, should be written in business-letter format. Remind students that the first paragraph of a business letter should be written in a positive way. This is especially important for #3. In the letter of recommendation, encourage students to specify how long they have known the person they are recommending and under what circumstances. Number 6 should be written much as a student would write a persuasive essay—with a clear introduction and strong evidence to support the request.

Exercise 9.12 (p. 107)

Assignments 1 through 4 should show creativity and a sense of fun. Number 5 should be approached seriously. Most authors (or their representatives) will answer correspondence in response to a real question. Send letters to the authors in care of their publishers, whose addresses can be found on the copyright pages of books or through a library.

Exercise 9.13 (p. 109)

Before students write responses to the essay questions, review terms like compare, contrast, explain, define, etc. Though student answers will vary, they all should respond to the directions. This may take practice, but it will be well worth it. In answering question 2, students may need help recognizing that "heart's treasury" refers to their bank of memories and that the final line means no thief is able to steal memories.

Name_____ Date _____

Glossary

alliteration—the use of the same letter or the same sound at the beginning of two or more words that are near to one another

audience—The person or persons for whom a writer is writing

brainstorming—allowing the free flow of words and/or ideas

clauses—contains a noun and a verb as well as other parts of speech

developing a paragraph—expanding the topic sentence of a paragraph with sentences that explain, tell a story, define, or give facts

developing sentences—expanding basic sentences made up of a verb, noun, or pronoun

editing—a two-step process in which the written material is first revised and then proofread. In the first step the writer is concerned with polishing the material, in the second, with correcting any errors.

essay—a group of paragraphs supporting a thesis statement (a clear statement of the subject to be explored). Essays are usually written in a formal style.

essay question—test question that requires sentence responses

figurative language—language that is not to be interpreted word for word; the opposite of literal language

final draft—the final draft of a manuscript incorporating all the changes and corrections made in the editing process

imagery—figurative language that appeals to the senses

irony—figurative language in which the literal meaning is the opposite of the author's intended meaning

journal—a written record of events, thoughts, or ideas, often written in the first person

literal language—language that is to be interpreted word for word; the opposite of figurative language

metaphor—a figure of speech, that implies a comparison between two quite different things

narrative—a story or the retelling of a sequence of events, either real or fictional

onomatopoeia—the use of words that sound like or suggest the objects or actions being named

outline—a graphic way to structure ideas by listing main points as major headings and supporting materials as subheads under the appropriate major headings

paragraph—a group of sentences linked together by common ideas

121   *Writing: A Comprehensive Guide to the Writing Process*

Name_____   Date_____

personification—figurative language in which the writer gives human qualities to an animal or inanimate object

prepositional phrase—phrase that begins with a preposition and ends with a noun or pronoun. Prepositional phrases can be used to expand sentences.

proofreading—a step in the writing process in which the writer corrects spelling and grammar

purpose—the reason the writer is writing. It may be to inform, to convince, to entertain, or to inform. Some writing will combine all these purposes.

revising—a step in the writing process in which the writer polishes the written piece

rough draft—a writer's first, unpolished attempt to arrange sentences into paragraphs organized around a main idea

simile—compares two things using the words "like" or "as"

slang—informal language, often quite colorful, usually relatively specific to a certain time, place, and group of people

topic sentence—a sentence that tells your reader what you plan to write about in a paragraph

transitional words—words that carry the reader smoothly from one sentence or paragraph to the next

web—a graphic organizer, often used as part of brainstorming

writing process—a plan to follow in order to reach a writing goal

Share Your Bright Ideas with Us!

We want to hear from you! Your valuable comments and suggestions will help us meet your current and future classroom needs.

Your name_____Date_____

School name_____Phone_____

School address_____

Grade level taught_____Subject area(s) taught_____Average class size_____

Where did you purchase this publication?_____

Was your salesperson knowledgeable about this product?   Yes_____   No_____

What monies were used to purchase this product?

____School supplemental budget   ____Federal/state funding   ____Personal

Please "grade" this Walch publication according to the following criteria:

Quality of service you received when purchasing .... A   B   C   D   F

Ease of use.. A   B   C   D   F

Quality of content... A   B   C   D   F

Page layout .... A   B   C   D   F

Organization of material .... A   B   C   D   F

Suitability for grade level .... A   B   C   D   F

Instructional value.. A   B   C   D   F

COMMENTS:_____

_____

What specific supplemental materials would help you meet your current—or future—instructional needs?

_____

Have you used other Walch publications? If so, which ones?_____

May we use your comments in upcoming communications?   ____Yes   ____No

Please **FAX** this completed form to **207-772-3105**, or mail it to:

Product Development, J.Weston Walch, Publisher, P.O. Box 658, Portland, ME 04104-0658

We will send you a **FREE GIFT** as our way of thanking you for your feedback.   **THANK YOU!**